ESCAPE FROM NORTH KOREA

A DESPERATE QUEST FOR FOOD, LOVE AND LIFE

Paul Estabrooks

Open *Doors*

Serving persecuted **Christians** worldwide

Dedicated to the faithful Korean Christians

of China who risk their lives helping

North Korean refugees...

...and to the memory of

those many refugees who have been

sent back to North Korea to a horrific fate.

PERSONALITIES IN THIS TRUE STORY

Pil Soo Kim – main character who later changed his name to Peter.

Myung Hee Kim – Pil Soo's wife who later changed her name to Maria.

Sung Yeon Kim – Pil Soo's daughter whose name was changed to Sharon.

Dae Jin Kim – Pil Soo's son whose name was later changed to Daniel.

Grandmother Kim – Pil Soo's aged mother who died of uterine cancer in China.

Kyung Jo Park – Pil Soo's best friend while in North Korea.

Elder Cha – Christian Korean-Chinese refugee worker and missionary.

Esther Li – Korean-Chinese Christian house church pastor.

Miriam Li – Esther Li's daughter.

Pastor James Lee – Korean pastor who works with the North Korean refugee "Underground Railway" enabling North Koreans to find their way to South Korea via China and Mongolia or South-east Asia.

Kim Il Sung – The founding "Great Leader" of the Democratic People's Republic of Korea (popularly known as North Korea) since 1948. Born April 15, 1912, Kim Il Sung died July 8, 1994. He is designated in the constitution as the country's "Eternal President." His birthday and the anniversary of his death are still public holidays in North Korea.

Kim Jong-il – Son of Kim Il Sung born February 16,

1941. He is currently the president of North Korea and known locally as "Dear Leader."

Soon Ok Lee – Ms. Lee survived six years of brutal treatment in North Korean prisons and managed to escape from North Korea in 1996. She documents the plight of Christian prisoners in North Korea in her book, *The Eyes of the Tailless Animals*. See Recommended Reading.

INTRODUCTION

The history of the Korean peninsula jutting out from the continent of Asia goes back almost 5,000 years. Resistance to outside influences, especially from the three powerful surrounding nations, China, Japan and Russia, significantly characterized those millennia. Today North Korea is still known as "the Hermit Kingdom."

On August 11, 1945, as World War II was coming to an end, the Korean peninsula was divided by an invisible line—the 38th Parallel. For the previous thirty-five years, Korea had been forcibly occupied by Japan, and most Koreans thought that their long awaited independence had finally arrived. However, they were faced with another disappointment. The nation was divided and occupied by troops from the world's two superpowers: the Soviet Union in the north and America in the south. Initially, the purpose of both the Soviet and American occupations in Korea was to establish military rule in their respective zones until a Korean government was formed.

Five years later, on June 15, 1950, North Korean communist troops invaded the south with the goal of "reuniting the fatherland." The invaders were strongly backed by Russia and China. The resulting war lasted more than three years. On July 27, 1953, the Korean War was suspended by an armistice agreement. But the 38th Parallel continues to divide the Korean people to this day.

South Korea—officially the Republic of Korea—established a democratic government. North Korea became formally known as The Democratic People's Republic of Korea and was led by a despot, Kim Il Sung. It is one of the most repressive countries in the world, allowing absolutely no political or religious freedoms. It annually tops Open Doors' World Watch List of restrictive nations. For the purpose of simplicity, we will refer to the two countries as North Korea and South Korea.

The Christian church began in Korea about 120 years ago. Unlike today, it was stronger in the north than in the south. At the outset of the Korean War, many Christians in the north fled to the south, but vast numbers were trapped in the north. A frightening number of Christians in North Korea have paid the ultimate sacrifice by standing up for their faith.

In recent years, Open Doors' researchers have confirmed that since October of 1999, dozens of Christians have been killed in public by firing squads. All were young in the faith, members of a first generation of new converts. Most were Koreans who became Christians while in China and were eager to share the Gospel with people back in their homeland. Young converts like these are the most vulnerable in North Korea, whereas older second and third generation Christians seem to know what it takes to survive.

In May 1997, seven imprisoned North Korean Christians in Hambuk Province had their jaws broken by guards because they continued to pray and sing praises to God. Minutes later they were shot to death.

Other incidents, again in Hambuk prison, took place in March and July of 1998. Four Christians were shot to death. In an effort to force one prisoner to deny his faith in Jesus Christ, guards starved him for days. When he refused to give in, he was shot to death. Three other prisoners displayed remarkable boldness and peace concerning their faith. North Korean officers beat them severely until they became unconscious. Then they were shot.

In December 1999, two ladies were openly shot in Haesan city on charges of illegal smuggling. In reality they were faithful Christians and ministered actively. During the same month two other Christians were shot in public in Hambuk Province. One of them had every tooth broken so that he could not talk clearly. Yet he boldly witnessed and preached the gospel to the end—even as he was being dragged to the place of execution.

These heartrending testimonies are only the tip of the iceberg. At least twenty Christians were arrested for their faith in 2004. According to reliable sources, tens of thousands of Christians are currently in North Korean prison camps, where they are suffering all sorts of inhuman cruelties. It is also believed that North Korea detains more political and religious prisoners than any other nation. Though no all-encompassing figures can be obtained, it is known that during the past year more than twenty Christians were killed in open-air shootings or by beatings in prison camps.

The plight of Christian workers from outside is also atrocious, even in neighbouring China. Two South Korean pastors and two laymen were imprisoned in China in April of 2002 because of their pastoral and humanitarian work among North Korean refugees. One remains in prison at this writing.

Though the two Koreas share nearly 5,000 years of history, they have been separated from each other for the past fifty years. This book, however, is about neither Korean politics nor Korean history. Nor is it a commentary on the economic situation of the countries, even though North Korea's economic output per person is estimated at only six percent of South Korea's annual, per-person output of $17,300.

This is a true story about a family that lived under the

North Korean regime, and their almost unbelievable experiences while escaping from it. All the names in this book are pseudonyms to protect identities and ministries. Peter and Maria Kim gave permission to tell their story because none of their immediate family is left in North Korea. Most North Korean refugees have relatives back in their homeland, so their stories remain untold for security reasons.

The sumptuous meals described by Peter while in China may seem unrealistic. Just remember they are the memories of a man who was essentially starving.

My deepest thanks are due to two close Korean friends who helped significantly with the interviewing and research of this story. Unfortunately, for security reasons they also cannot be named.

Sincere appreciation also goes to the Korean brothers and sisters of The Light Korean Presbyterian Church in Toronto, Canada, who helped with translation to English of lengthy Korean language interview tapes.

Special thanks to Herman Weiskopf for his invaluable help in the writing of this manuscript and to Nita Kellner for her sharp-eyed copy editing.

Paul Estabrooks
Minister-at-large
Open Doors International
March 2006

CHAPTER 1

IS FOOD WORTH DYING FOR?

Pil Soo Kim stood semi-naked in the frigid, waist-high river, holding his clothes in his arms to keep them dry. The Tumen River was so much colder than he thought it would be, and it made breathing difficult. His legs slowly went numb, but not before the pain cut through them like a knife. It was already winter and the river had begun to freeze. For the moment, the pain from the glacial midnight temperatures masked the strong hunger pangs that drove him forward.

He shivered more from his freezing fear than the water. *"Is a border policeman watching me through his binoculars?"* Pil Soo wondered. He could not turn back now for fear of being captured by the North Korean border patrol. But he worried too about the Chinese patrols on the other side. Were they also observing him and just waiting for him to come ashore?

So many other questions flooded his troubled mind. *"If I get caught, am I ever going to get home? What will happen to my family?"*

Just minutes earlier, as he was hiding and waiting for the signal to cross the river, he began to have mixed feelings about this trip. First he felt guilty, as if he were a traitor to his country. Though he resented the recent changes and the widespread hunger, North Korea was still his homeland. But love for country lost out to love for a family desperately in need of food and something, anything that could give substance and purpose to life. Etched in his mind forever were haunting memories of his father, two brothers and a sister—all of whom had died of starvation or from illnesses they were too weak to fight off. He would not let that be the fate of the remainder of his family.

If caught by Chinese or North Korean police or soldiers, one of two fates awaited him: life in jail or death. That danger was accentuated by memories of a friend who had gone to China to earn money by selling homegrown mushrooms. He was caught and promptly executed. Local residents in China and North Korea are sometimes forced by the authorities to witness such atrocities, the better to ensure that the masses would be sufficiently terror-stricken.

Pil Soo did not fear so much for his own life, but he was worried about his family if he failed. They would suffer severely because of his activity—even be sent to labor camp by the National Security Agency.

Many times people were shot while crossing the river, and their dead bodies just left there. He had heard that children once swam across the polluted Tumen River, then collapsed and died. The thought that he might be stepping over a dead body right now terrified him. He had heard too many stories about them floating along the shoreline. Since it was the middle of the night, he could not see anything. Maybe it was better this way.

Danger was always present in crossing the border illegally. But there was no other way. This was his last resort. He could not take his mind off his family at home. Pil Soo half-smiled as he pictured them sleeping at night, without pain from an empty stomach. For this he was even willing to die. It was all about food and it started years earlier.

CHAPTER 2

SPECIAL FOOD DAY

Pil Soo held his card high above his head as he marched down the huge square in Pyongyang, North Korea's capital city. All he could see beyond his uplifted arms were neatly lined rows of other Korean people to his left and right, as well as directly ahead. They too marched smartly as they proudly held their cards high. Pil Soo could not see the total effect, but he knew he was just one small part of a massive picture of their "Great Leader".

It was April 15, 1994, Kim Il Sung's birthday, known locally as "Sun Day." North Korea traces its beginning to this day in 1912 when Kim Il Sung was born. School children have since been reminded often and at length about how magnificent a man he was, and how he made it possible for them to have such glorious lives. But the thousand or more people who had died of starvation overnight did not share those thoughts.

There were cheering sections of students as well as a

grand choir. The students participating practiced until midnight for days in advance. As Pil Soo turned over his card at exactly the same moment as his companions, the big picture became the flag of North Korea, an intricate design with blue stripes at top and bottom, plus a red center into which was incorporated a white circle that housed a red five-point star.

The watching audience excitedly warmed the square with their expressions of awe. Pil Soo wished that warmth could help him, because he was freezing. This year the government had given everyone a new uniform with short sleeve shirts. They were made in prison factories. But the weather had taken a turn for the worse and the wind chill factor was bitter.

"This is torture," he muttered quietly to himself. Yet he had actually volunteered for this duty today. It was a special honor to be part of the celebrations in the capital, rather than just in his hometown. He had made certain his own national flag was flying from the doorpost before he left home early that morning.

His empty stomach rumbled because it had been a long time since breakfast. His wife, Myung Hee, had prepared him a small serving of *congee* (porridge) made from powdered corn meal. It tasted something like potatoes, a flavor he loved. Even on this special holiday there was not a trace of the favorite Korean *kimchee*. This, the national dish of all Korea, consists of a pickled vegetable seasoned with garlic, red pepper and ginger.

Pil Soo salivated as he imagined the taste of the special treats he might be enjoying in a few hours. Most of all, he anticipated receiving an egg in addition to cigarettes, cooking oil and cornmeal. This was a yearly tradition and the treats were highlights of the "Great Leader's" birthday for every-one—especially the children, who also received candies and cookies.

He shivered from the cold and continued to march in step with the others. With every pace, he counted down the seconds until the parade would be over, and he could take the train home and join his family at their local sporting events. There would be soccer, volleyball and basketball games as well as foot races and even hoola-hoop performances. Usually they lasted for two days, but this year there would only be one day of sports. Rumors were circulating that the country was experiencing financial difficulties which surpassed any in years gone by.

But first he knew they all would have to listen to some very long, boring speeches. Most people hated them, but they were an indispensable part of the birthday tribute. And worse, everyone was expected to memorize the "Great Leader's" speech that day.

Pil Soo kept rubbing his hands over his chilled arms and chest while speakers droned on and on, exalting Kim Il Sung. He shivered so hard from the cold, he thought he was having convulsions. He passed the slowly moving time by dreaming again of good food.

But the food was not to be a reality this year. For the first time in his life and memory, the birthday events ended with no special food treats. Just the children received a two-pound bag of hard candies and cookies. Some of them looked impossible to eat.

As the train sped across the countryside toward his hometown, Pil Soo stared dejectedly out the window. Lately it seemed disappointment was the staple of life in North Korea.

CHAPTER 3

ALL ABOUT FOOD

Months later Pil Soo trudged down the dusty narrow road toward his home, staring at the ground. He no longer even noticed the huge Kim Il Sung photo-billboard on the corner with the message, **"KIM IL SUNG IS WITH YOU ALWAYS."** Pil Soo had stopped glancing at that sign months earlier, when he had come to realize it was time to admit that none of the "Great Leader's" robust promises of prosperity and plates full of food ever came true.

Reaching that conclusion had first made him feel uncomfortable and then like a traitor. It had been pounded into his head thousands of times that he was indebted to the "Great Leader" for all he had. Whenever he considered the words, *"all I have,"* or mentioned them to others, he chuckled. As time wore on, however, that slight humor was replaced by resentment and bitterness, for he knew all too well that the broken promises had dire implications for his family and his country.

Any onlooker would have thought Pil Soo was suffering from a very heavy heart. What was actually bothering him was some kind of sickness. He could not understand how he could feel so good yesterday and so awful today. His stomach was aching and diarrhea was threatening again. He wondered if he had caught the same bug Myung Hee, his wife, had just recovered from. The doctor had called it paratyphus.

"Why did we have to buy a house so far out on the edge of town?" he complained to himself as he dragged his feet down the road. He knew the answer as well as anyone. Houses cost a lot of money these days. And he did not have the resources for a better one, or for a house with a central location in this steel town in the mountains. He well remembered the struggle to acquire his little three-room unit. It had no roof, so he built one. Then adding all the little changes Myung Hee wanted kept him very busy, not to speak of the time assembling all the furniture in their home. The floor was cement, covered with yellow paper that he had acquired from a factory. They couldn't afford vinyl floor tiles from China.

"You're home from work early again! Did you have any lunch?" Myung Hee exclaimed as he entered the house and flopped down on a chair. Pil Soo did not need to answer the second question. She would have been surprised if he answered affirmatively.

He had a good job as a carpenter at a furniture factory and earned an average salary—fifty *won* a month (approximately five to seven US dollars equivalent). But furniture supplies were scarce so the hours of work were also few. Some days most workers did not even show up. Pil Soo only worked about ten days a month. His being home early did not surprise Myung Hee at all, but his pained expressions did.

"Oh, I'm so sick I feel like I'm going to die. I left work early because my fever is really high. Maybe I'll be an addition to the fifty or so of our town's people dying today! Then you can eat my body," Pil Soo replied in all seriousness. That was a reality in their area. But no one openly talked about it. Two sons of a nearby neighbor had recently starved to death. Surprisingly, there had been no funeral. Rumors were rampant. It was too close to home!

"Nonsense," retorted Myung Hee. "You've just got a cold again, from this changing weather! Come lie down on the bed and I'll get you some hot water to drink." On the one hand, she sought to downplay her husband's condition; on the other, she inwardly fretted about his pain and fever.

"How was your day?" Pil Soo grimaced as he held his aching stomach.

"Nothing more notable than neighbors begging for food again! Of course, I had nothing for them. The Soon family thinks their Grandma may die of hunger tonight. She regularly insists her grandchildren be given her portion of food."

"Where's my mother?" Pil Soo queried as he looked around the cottage for their resident grandmother. He frowned as the side-by-side photos of Kim Il Sung and his son, Kim Jong-il, looked down from their prominent place on the largest wall. They were a constant reminder to him of the source of North Korea's food problems.

"Oh she's gone to the mountainside to gather grass to make porridge. The children went with her. They'll try and find some pine tree bark also."

"You mean we're out of corn rice again already," Pil Soo replied in a tone of frustration.

"Yes," Myung Hee responded softly. She did not want to burden him in his weakened state, but he had to know the truth. "Our rations don't go very far anymore."

"I hope Mother doesn't come down with another case of poison ivy out there today," he interjected. "Last time, just watching her scratch her rash made me feel like I also had it."

"And Pil Soo," she continued as though she did not hear him. "Your mother is so disappointed she can't set up a noodle shop. She talks about nothing else. Especially when the neighbors are constantly begging us for food. Just when she thinks she has enough money, some major expenses come along. She's still saved only about half of what she would need to start a business."

Pil Soo felt so badly that he could not help his mother adequately fulfill her dreams. But then, what about Myung Hee's dreams? And those of his children Sung Yeon and Dae Jin? Not to mention his own. And now Grandma was hitting bottom, picking grass and bark from the mountainside to make soup. Even though he felt sick to his stomach, the thought of some grass soup revived his spirits ever so slightly. But it would be hours before the soup was ready, and that would be all the family had for their evening meal.

"If only..." Pil Soo started.

"We can't survive on broken dreams," Myung Hee broke in. "It's not your fault those officers did not make good on their promise to pay."

Pil Soo just shrugged and wished he could forget. It made his stomach hurt even more when he recalled those five officers. A year ago, he and Myung Hee had decided to take a big risk and start a private business, something that was forbidden in North Korea. After careful planning, they went to the east coast to Myung Hee's birth town and purchased some squid and crabs and sold them for a good profit in their hometown. After purchasing food for themselves, they used the rest of the money to buy Chinese products from the "open" market. These Chinese items cost ten times the price of local goods. They then sold them in Myung Hee's east coast birth town for a profit—again returning home with seafood and rice and corn.

But recently five uniformed officers appeared at their door. Neighbors had apparently reported that Pil Soo and Myung Hee were a source of good food. Someone was always informing in this society. The five men promised to pay them if they put on a good feed. Myung Hee went all out, serving Grandma's great noodle soup and fresh bread and wine that she had used all their savings to purchase from the market place. The men promised to return that night with a one hundred-pound-bag of rice as payment for their feast. As was true of the "Great Leader", that promise was never kept.

The next day the neighborhood committee of the Communist Party held a criticism meeting against Pil Soo's capitalistic ventures, and penalized him with a stiff fine. Pil Soo felt they were motivated by jealousy more than ideology. But now he was financially way behind, and there would be no more trips to the east coast—especially if this sickness did not improve. The more Pil Soo searched for a purpose in life, the more he concluded that there wasn't one. There was absolutely no way out of this pointless existence.

"Maybe we'll have to sell the house," Pil Soo said in a voice that startled him with its loudness. "It should be worth four thousand *won* now!"

"And where will your family live then?" Myung Hee wanted to know.

"Well, we could rent a very small place near the market, and Mother could start her noodle shop." Pil Soo's strength slowly seeped out of his body and he soon was too weak to even talk.

Upon her arrival at the house, Pil Soo's mother needed only to take a quick look at him and feel his forehead to know that her son needed help. Hurriedly, she created some of her special potions, ones that in the past had cured all manner of ailments. That night, though, no cure was found. Pil Soo's fever raged on.

After four days of fever, Pil Soo gradually recovered; but his resolve to improve the lot of his family did not weaken. He knew he had to take some big risks if they were going to survive.

CHAPTER 4

My Decision Is Made

From early childhood on, North Koreans are taught that their lifestyle is the best on earth. But an increasing number of the people are concluding that life in their country is one of such despair and hopelessness, that it all too closely resembles a living death. Malnutrition is rampant, so much so that a modification had to be made in the minimum height allowable for males to enter the army. As a result of the stunted growth of the downtrodden masses, the minimum height was lowered from five feet five inches to five feet two inches.

Empty stomachs prevail among all but a few elite. Current President Kim Jong-il has repeatedly promised his people that lives will soon improve; that jobs, fine homes and happiness are on the horizon. That horizon has never materialized. It has all added up to this: everyone is scared of dying and yet everyone fears living. That's why Pil Soo was convinced that he had to put his plan into action. As he lay in bed on the night he made up his mind, he was surprised—even strengthened—by the realization that he was deriving comfort from the words, "My decision is made." And so it was that a tossing-turning sleep finally embraced him.

As much as he wanted to share his resolve with his wife Myung Hee, this was not possible. First of all, she would almost certainly try to talk him out of going to China. And, if she consented to his going, she would be terrified about the dangers he would have to face. So Pil Soo proceeded cautiously—and alone.

His first step was to visit his closest friend, Kyung Jo, who had already told him that he could put him in touch with guides for the journey. Even this seemingly routine step was not without its risks, for there had been more than a few incidents in which trusted friends had alerted authorities, who captured or killed would-be escapees. Friends who turned against friends did so because any association with anyone who wanted to flee to China immediately endangered themselves.

Over and over, Pil Soo battled fears that gnawed at him and tried to put holes in his project. He kept winning those confrontations by reciting what was becoming his mantra: "my decision is made." But when he visited Kyung Jo it was his friend who was overcome by fear, so much so that he tried to convince Pil Soo to abandon his mission. Kyung Jo consented to put him in touch with the guides only when he became convinced of Pil Soo's total commitment.

A few days later Pil Soo met with the guides, a woman in her early forties and her tall, muscular teenage son. They had made numerous trips across the Tumen River that divides northeast North Korea and northeast China. Their first caution to him was that it was November, and that meant that the river would be almost unbearably cold. Before entering the water, they explained, all clothes except for underwear would be rolled up and carried overhead so that they had dry clothing when they reached the Chinese border. Wet clothes, the son stressed, would mark them as river crossers, a perception they had to avoid.

In November, the Tumen River begins to freeze and the border patrol is less intense because of the cold weather. The reality is that many people still cross the river despite the frigid water and the security risk.

Once in China, they would walk several miles to a safe house, where they would be fed and where they would stay overnight. The hosts, the guides pointed out, were experienced in all of this. In the morning, the three would take a bus to a nearby city and then separate. The guides would conduct their usual business, and Pil Soo would try to find a man who, a year or so ago, had promised to assist him if ever he made it to China. Three days later, they would all meet at the city bus terminal. The guides' instructions, advice, expertise and warnings were so explicit that they gave Pil Soo a legitimate assurance that his plan was going to work.

The guides had arranged for them to begin their trip three days later, by meeting shortly before midnight at a designated spot along the river. Payment to the guides would consist of one-third of all the food and money Pil Soo was able to acquire. Half of that would go to a relative of the guides, who would be the guard on duty the night of their crossing. Payment would also have to be made to owners of the safe house.

On his way back home from that meeting, Pil Soo considered everything he had heard and almost decided to cancel out. After all, how much food could he bring back from China? And there was no shortage of tales about escapees who were caught and unmercifully persecuted or about how their bullet-riddled bodies floated down the Tumen River. Besides, his only meeting with the Korean-Chinese gentleman he was counting on for help had been a hello-goodbye affair. His lone consolation was that Kyung Jo had told him this man, Elder Cha, had aided other North Koreans, and that he could be relied on for everything. He and a co-worker would house Pil Soo, feed him, give him food and even provide him with money, declared his friend. It sounded too good to be true, but if Kyung Jo said it was so, then it was so.

One huge drawback was that Pil Soo had no way of letting Elder Cha know that he would be coming. In the end, he blocked out all such negatives by repeating to himself, "My decision is made. But what if...."

"My decision is made. My decision is made."

CHAPTER 5

UNBELIEVABLE FOOD

It was almost time to cross the Tumen River. As he crouched down in the long grass on a hill overlooking the riverbank, Pil Soo felt that his senses had never been keener. Despite the darkness, he was able to spot all sorts of things, even the way the grass was bent by the slight wind that prevailed.

While preparing mentally for this evening, Pil Soo had repeatedly reminded himself to be on the lookout for *anything* that could endanger him. In a very real way, he was going to entrust his life into the hands of two people he had known for no more than two hours. What if they had set him up to be captured? That was a definite possibility, for he didn't have money to pay the guides up front, and he could only trust their word that they were willing to wait for their money until the return trip. What if something went wrong, and the relative or other guards spotted him in the river and gleefully used him for target practice? Then came his solace. "My decision is made."

His head snapped sharply to the left in response to movement. Sure enough, someone was there, ten or fifteen yards away. More rustling. Now he was beginning to pick up the outlines of two figures approaching him. Pil Soo readied himself to run if they were not the guides. Within a minute, the two people were close enough for him to recognize the woman and her son.

The guides knelt down in silence, one on either side of Pil Soo. He could see the flashlight in the woman's right hand and knew that she was waiting for the precise moment when it would be time to signal the guard. After a wait of a few minutes, that was exactly what she did, allowing the beam to stay on for just a flicker. Two seconds later came the flick of a flashlight from the guard on patrol—the signal that the way was clear for them to enter the water.

Slowly, gingerly, catlike, they inched down the slope. Ten feet from the river the guides disrobed, and wrapped their clothes and shoes into bundles. Pil Soo did likewise. Clad only in his underwear, he now felt that, as minimal as the wind was, it added a distinct bite to the cold air. There was no time to fret about that, for the woman and her son were moving more swiftly than he had anticipated. They remained crouched as they entered the water, each with a bundle overhead, and then stood more and more erect as the river deepened.

The guides had chosen a strategic place to make their entry, a spot where the river was less than forty yards across and where they could enter without making a splash. Halfway across, the water was only up to Pil Soo's waist. Occasionally he struggled with his balance because, as he realized, walking with his hands over his head for the first time in his life encumbered him. When the water reached his chest, he had to pause to catch his breath and remind himself that he didn't dare to make a sound.

The first twenty yards went fairly fast, followed by a slowdown as Pil Soo's body labored from being so long in the coldest water it had ever been subjected to. And then, there came into view the first glimpse of the Chinese side of the river. A burst of confidence and exhilaration swept over him. They were going to make it into China.

Indeed they did. Then they wriggled their wet bodies into their dry clothes and shoes. After that it was time for a brisk walk of more than two hours, to the safe house and a couple who had been used by the guides on all their previous journeys. This husband and wife, like the guides, were willing to wait for their payment from Pil Soo.

Every effort was made to remain inconspicuous during the walk. Just because they did not see any uniformed policemen or soldiers did not mean they were safe; especially since Chinese officials were known to employ bounty hunters, who earned their living by nabbing North Koreans smuggled across the border.

The owners of the safe house had received notice that the three were coming at this hour, so they were prepared. Warm greetings, a warm house and a warm bed added up to a perfect end to Pil Soo's evening.

Following a short sleep, Pil Soo sat down with the guides and the owners for breakfast. There was so much food that he commented, "This is not a breakfast. This is a banquet."

"Eat up," said the host, with a resounding laugh.

Eat he did. Several courses were served and everyone took large helpings. The centerpiece of the meal was a beef stew, a treat Pil Soo had never eaten. From the first bite of that stew to the last, he kept telling himself he had never eaten anything quite so tasty. He couldn't help thinking, *"If only my family were here to enjoy this delicious food."* He became so engrossed in this notion that tears actually rolled down his cheeks and landed in his bowl of rice. The ever-discreet host turned away so that Pil Soo would have a chance to wipe his face.

"You're thinking about your wife and children, right?" asked the host. "Don't be so sad. Have more food. When everything is over, your family will also have plenty of food."

Before Pil Soo left for the next leg of this adventure, the host gave him information about which bus to take to the city where he was to meet Elder Cha. First, though, came a half-hour walk to the bus station, where he and the guides chose a spot where they would meet in three days. The woman and her son then boarded a bus that would take them south to the city where their contacts lived. When their bus pulled away, Pil Soo was shaken by the realization that he was not only alone, but that he was alone in a foreign country. Minutes later, he boarded another bus for a three-hour trip.

Never had he seen a bus like this. From his seat near the back he marveled at how clean the bus was, and that it was equipped with television for riders to watch. While watching that TV set, Pil Soo was shocked to see advertisements in which Chinese women wore nothing more than their under garments. Nothing so promiscuous was ever seen in North Korea.

Roughly an hour into his ride, Pil Soo's mind began to wander. There were thoughts about his family, about how good and kind the guides and hosts had been to him, and about how seamlessly this mission had gone so far. Up to this point, each step had been built on the experience of those around him. Now would come a venture into the unknown, since no one knew that he was arriving. He didn't even know if Elder Cha would be available, or if the man would remember who he was. Pil Soo had only the vaguest recollection of what this Elder Cha looked like, except that he was tall, slightly stooped and probably in his mid-fifties.

*****

That's why he began pulling out all his memories of how they had met. It went back almost a year, to a day when Pil Soo visited his pal Kyung Jo. They had known each other since childhood, and their times together were invariably pleasant. That day, though, much of their conversation centered on news that increasing numbers of North Koreans had been able to filter their way into China and return with food and money. Some took goods they would sell. Others, Kyung Jo said, were able to contact people in China—mostly Koreans who had been born in China—who had set up networks enabling people to continue their escape route all the way into South Korea.

Pil Soo was intrigued and his questions tumbled out.

Kyung Jo answered, "Most of those helpers are Christians who put their lives on the line to aid others. It is incredible, what God is doing in all of this. You speak of your despair, and how you worry about your family's well being. Nothing is going to improve this country under this dictatorship, and that's why so many are fleeing.

"It's worth a try. I can put you in touch with excellent guides who have much experience in making trips to China.

What do you think?"

Pil Soo's mouth dropped open as he listened to his friend. He had never heard Kyung Jo mention God and he had no idea that his buddy knew anything about border crossings. That's why it took him about thirty seconds before he said, "I don't know what to think." And then he fell silent.

As Kyung Jo spoke more and more about God and His son, Jesus, Pil Soo became increasingly bewildered. In all his life he had only heard a few mentions of God and Jesus. They were strangers to him. How could he put trust in strangers? Had his friend gone off the deep end?

"Please come back tonight to meet Elder Cha," Kyung Jo said. "I am not yet able to explain a great deal to you about God and Jesus, but Elder Cha can. He helped me invite them into my life. This man has come from his home in northeast China again, and is staying with me this time. Elder Cha does much to assist those who wish to escape to China and beyond. He also brings with him Bibles printed in Korean, and distributes them to people here. Right now, he is not here. But he will return in a few hours."

Religious activities—even conversations—are banned in North Korea, where anyone caught indulging faces harsh penalties. Against his better judgment, Pil Soo consented to return at six o'clock.

On the way home—and once there—he contemplated all that he had heard. Kyung Jo, who was normally restrained at all times, had been animated and gleeful when talking about some sort of religion that he had "accepted into" his life. None of that made sense.

In trying to cover all eventualities, Pil Soo went so far as to consider the possibility that Kyung Jo was baiting a trap for him. In the end, he decided to return to his friend's home so that his curiosity about several matters—more than anything, about smuggling his way into China and back—could be satisfied. And then there was Kyung Jo's enthusiasm when he spoke about God. *Who* was God? *What* was God? Had God given Kyung Jo something that made him so joyous?

Pil Soo's waffling had consumed considerable time, so much so that he was two hours late arriving at Kyung Jo's house. That was unfortunate, for Elder Cha was almost ready to depart. At the end of the few minutes that he had to spare, this dignified-looking gentleman looked Pil Soo in the eyes, handed him a slip of paper and said, "Here, take this. It's my address and phone number. If you ever come to China, look me up. I understand that you two have discussed some serious topics."

Pil Soo had no idea how to respond, except to express his thanks, though he wasn't sure what for. Elder Cha, in his final words to him, said, "God loves you, and He has a wonderful plan for your life. I will pray that you will find His plan and fulfill it."

That left Pil Soo more confused than ever.

After Elder Cha departed, Kyung Jo, who was new to the Christian faith, made valiant efforts to explain how and why he had placed his trust in Jesus. Stuff about sins and forgiveness and heaven. It all sounded like gibberish to Pil Soo, who could not grasp the meanings of religious words and concepts. Twenty minutes of such talk were all he could handle. He knew he had to get out of the house and away from his friend; so he did, all the while offering apologies and thanks.

Off and on during the next several days, questions

popped into his mind concerning that evening's peculiar turn of events. *"Who is this God and where is He?"* Pil Soo wondered. *"What did He do to Kyung Jo? What can He do for me? What does it mean to 'believe' in Him? How can I believe in someone I cannot see or hear? Why is my friend so ecstatic about this 'relationship' he has with Jesus, whoever he is? I want to believe Kyung Jo, but it's impossible to figure out what he is saying."*

*****

Pil Soo almost had to shake himself back to reality. He had heard that the Chinese lived far better than North Korean people and he saw lots of evidence to support that, as he looked out the bus window. He thought that the house where he had stayed overnight was one of the finest he had ever seen. Yet as the bus approached his destination, Pil Soo noticed house after house that was bigger and fancier. *"How can so many people have so much money to afford these houses?"* he thought. As the bus neared the city, he was dazzled by the buildings there, almost all of which were decorated with neon lights or colorful banners or signs. It was easy to sense that this was a nation where there was vitality. And the people he saw in the terminal, on the bus and on the streets had such purpose in their stride.

As he meandered through the terminal, he put his right hand into his pants pocket for what must have been the twentieth time since leaving home. Sure enough, the slip of paper that Elder Cha had given him was still there. Pil Soo was well aware that he was now entering another level of being on his own. He could not ask just anyone for directions, for he did not understand Chinese. His hope rested in spotting a Chinese-born Korean. Although this was successfully accomplished, and although the couple gave him detailed directions, Pil Soo could not comprehend what they told him, because he was not familiar with the city or the names of the streets. And their accent was so different! He was in a quandary. Fortunately, he had planned for such a situation, so he fished in his pocket for coins he had been given at the safe house. Carefully he pulled out the slip of paper and telephoned Elder Cha.

To Pil Soo's amazement, the elder answered. What's more, he clearly recalled their brief time together. He advised Pil Soo not to stay in the bus station, because it was a favorite place for the secret police to look for North Korean escapees. Instead, Elder Cha gave him directions that would take him to a nearby food store, where they could meet in approximately fifteen minutes.

Once again Pil Soo was dumbfounded, this time by the vast number of items on sale in the food store. As he made every effort to act like a real shopper, he roamed through entire aisles of breads, cookies, paper products, canned vegetables and items he had never seen. Then, somewhere between the bean sprouts and the snow peas, in the produce section, the two men met. In order not to attract attention, both acted as if this were nothing more than a casual meeting. With Elder Cha leading the way, the two walked past the seemingly end-less array of fresh vegetables and out into the sunny, chilly early afternoon.

CHAPTER 6

OF BANANAS, ORANGES AND MORE

Within ten minutes, the two men entered a large house, where Elder Cha ushered Pil Soo to a seat on a plush sofa. Hardly had he sat down before he was back on his feet, being introduced by the elder to a woman named Esther, who was the owner of this tastefully furnished and decorated home. She and the elder were of Korean descent, had been born in China and spoke both languages fluently.

Esther explained briefly to Pil Soo that the elder had phoned her immediately after receiving his call, whereupon she and her daughter Miriam, who lived nearby, hastily put together a lunch for him. A lunch? This was another feast! Pil Soo gladly obeyed urgings from Esther and Elder Cha to, "Eat heartily."

Nothing amazed him more than a whole platter of chicken. "In North Korea, we eat chicken only at wedding receptions," he pointed out. "This is hard for me to believe."

Esther smiled at him and said, "Please believe it—and eat plenty of it."

The truth of the situation was that Pil Soo felt uneasy in this almost-elegant dining room and at a table laden with so much food. The hospitality of these people was hard for him to fathom. After all, he had never met either Esther or her daughter, and his acquaintance with the elder consisted of a mere few minutes. How could they be so gracious to a stranger from another land? And how could they afford to offer him so much food? But their gentle manner and sincere interest in who he was, and how his venture had gone thus far, made him feel welcome; and before the meal was finished, Pil Soo was already starting to feel at ease.

Still, he felt the need to ask a question: "How can you be so kind to me?"

It was the elder who chose to respond. "Since we met last year, I've been praying for you. Do you remember that when it was time for me to leave I said to you, 'God loves you and He has a plan for your life. I will pray that you find His plan and fulfill it'?"

Elder Cha's words did, indeed, have a familiar ring. But what they meant, especially the part about "prayer," was beyond Pil Soo's comprehension.

At that moment, Miriam placed two bowls of fruit on the table. Pil Soo had never seen two of the items before. "They're bananas and oranges," Esther told him. He devoured one of each and rolled his eyes as he sought to describe how much he enjoyed the fruit.

And then there came a platter of cookies. Some looked similar to ones in North Korean markets, but a quick sampling proved that they were of far better quality and taste.

It was colder than usual that evening, so Esther slipped outside and came back with a load of firewood. Pil Soo jumped up to give her a hand, and the two of them placed the wood in a stove located near the center of the living room. Soon the fire that had almost gone out was invigorated and warmed the room as Esther, Elder Cha and Pil Soo sat in comfortable easy chairs and drank ginseng tea. "This is the way life should be," Pil Soo thought.

For several minutes, the three sat silently. Pil Soo guessed that Esther was in her late fifties. She carried herself almost regally; yet, she had such a gentle way about her that it made everyone around her feel comfortable. Most women, he thought, would envy her naturally wavy hair. Esther had a small, soft face and smooth skin. Her large eyes radiated a rare kindness that manifested itself in all sorts of ways. She was an attractive woman who reminded him of an actress he had seen in a movie when he was a teen. Then it came to him. It was a movie called "Religious Shrine," which was about a Christian evangelist, a psychic and a Buddhist priest. Esther looked like one of the main characters.

While the others chatted, Pil Soo studied the elder. He was about six feet two inches tall, and had a long, narrow face; but his soft eyes could at times be piercing. His every movement was smooth, effortless, unhurried.

Pil Soo's mental picturing of the two ended abruptly when Elder Cha turned to him and said in his mellow voice, "I knew that one day we'd meet again."

"Why do you say that?" Pil Soo replied.

"The night you came to meet me in North Korea, you

had a look in your eyes that was different from the rest of the people God had put me in touch with there," the elder explained. "I've prayed for you every time you have come to mind, which has been quite often."

"What does it mean that you 'prayed' for me? Who do you pray to and why? What is prayer?" The questions that Pil Soo had been harboring spewed forth with a rush that startled and embarrassed him. Quickly, and somewhat awkwardly, he apologized to the elder, who did not say a word but smiled kindly, making Pil Soo feel forgiven and relieved.

"I pray—we pray—to God," Elder Cha began. "I prayed for God's will to be done in your life. If your coming to China is in His will, then I want to be part of it. Prayers are offered because they're our most eloquent way of communicating with God, and it's He who answers these prayers as He knows best. Many times He has proved to us that His love for us is constant and forever. Our prayers are not fancy, just conversations to give Him our thanks for all He has done and to bring to Him our needs and requests."

Elder Cha knew from previous situations that he had gone far enough. To continue, he had learned, would add to the confusion that was already going on in Pil Soo's mind.

Although Pil Soo could not understand much of what the elder had told him, he nodded as if he did. He did not want to disagree with someone who was so easy going and who might be instrumental in helping him while he was in China.

As for Esther, she had sipped her tea and nodded occasionally during the exchange between the men. "Tell us about yourself and your family," she now said to Pil Soo.

"I have a very beautiful wife, Myung Hee, and we have one son and one daughter. My mother also lives with us. My earliest memories are from my school days. I was not a good student—just an average student." In truth, he received below-average marks in elementary school, but he didn't want them to think poorly of him.

"In high school, however, I graduated with honors, because I had very good teachers and liked them. I was seventeen when I graduated. Actually, I never did graduate, because I had to join the army a month before graduation. I went into army training near the Demilitarized Zone (DMZ) between North and South Korea.

"It's mandatory to serve in the army for ten years. However, one mining town in the north desperately needed more workers; so Kim Il Sung ordered the army to send soldiers there, who'd grown up in the north, so they could work in the mines. Altogether, I was in the military service for nine years and retired at the age of twenty-six to work in those mines."

"What exactly did you do there?" Esther wanted to know.

"I was assigned to the part of the mining company that was overseeing all the industrial and residential construction in the northern provinces. We'd drills holes in huge rocks, insert dynamite and blow them into pieces, after which we'd sort out the stones. Only the stones that could be used for construction were saved. We had to dump the discards in the valley. Since there were only men working there, when the weather was warm we'd work in just our underwear."

Esther poured more tea for everyone. Much to Pil Soo's delight, she also offered a large plate filled with cookies. When he said, "These are sooooooo delicious," Esther and Elder Cha chuckled, for they could well imagine what a treat this was for him.

After wolfing down a few more cookies, Pil Soo picked up his words where he had left off. "I had to take a train from where I lived to where I worked, since it was far from our house. During the week, I lived at the work camp. We were all packed into small rooms in a dormitory that housed more than a hundred workers. We had many sanitation problems. There were fleas and lice, and we didn't have any insecticide to get rid of them. So during the day we would take our belongings outside to shake them out and clean them in any way we could.

"We were supposed to work an average of eight hours a day, but most of the time we worked longer. Sometimes we worked fewer hours because of problems with electricity. When that happened, and when the weather was so bad that we couldn't work, we played cards and gambled for food stamps or for money. There had been so many accidents and injuries on rainy days that work was called off when it rained.

"For breakfast we ate corn rice. For lunch we ate corn rice. For dinner we had noodle soup. Because the portions were so small, we were *always* hungry. Every fifteen days we were supposed to be given forty-five coupons to spend on meals at the camp, but we always came up short. That's why many of the men gambled for meal coupons."

"Wasn't that taking a terrible chance?" the elder asked. "I mean, whoever lost coupons would have even less food to eat."

"If they lost some coupons, it didn't really matter much because those people would be just a little hungrier than usual.

Everybody had to make a decision about whether or not he was willing to gamble. Meals cost two or three coupons, so we all learned how to live with stomachs that were never happy. For us, that was something we had become accustomed to."

When the cookie plate came around again, Pil Soo snatched up two of his favorite cookies. It was a good time to take a break, for he had been rambling on perhaps more than ever. He didn't know why he was talking so much, and sharing personal feelings with Esther and Elder Cha, except that in only a few hours he had created a precious bond with them. Usually, he was far more reserved and quiet in the presence of people he did not know well. But these two people's easygoing personalities and their sincere interest in what he said had motivated Pil Soo to keep on gabbing.

"When she was young, Myung Hee used to eat lots of apples, pears and peaches. When she was pregnant with our first child, she craved apples more than anything. When my father found out that we were not able to afford them, he somehow managed to bring her five apples. Myung Hee ate all five apples at one sitting, and everyone watched her and laughed as she refused to stop until she had eaten the last bite.

"My pay was so meager that it was impossible to give allowances to our children. Because of the economic situation at the time, a bottle of wine would cost about thirty *won* and one plate of tofu was about fifteen *won*. So, if you bought a bottle of wine and a plate of tofu, you had spent much of your month's salary. Also, one kilo of rice (a little more than two pounds) cost about eighty *won* and a kilo of barley cost fifty. After a full month of hard labor, you could buy only five hundred grams (one pound) of rice or a kilo of dry corn."

"It's amazing that you were able to survive on so little food," Esther said as she shook her head.

"That's true," Pil Soo said. "As the years of less and less food continue, starvation has increased. You have to learn how to live every day with a stomach that always complains. In addition to what rations the government gives us, and what we can earn, our family has learned how to make soup from grass and bark we find on the mountainside near our home. Such soup has little nourishment, but it has decent flavor and at least it is *something* to put in your belly.

"We have food stores where we can buy a variety of snacks. They are mostly products from China. However, the price is ten times more expensive than snacks made in North Korea because of the quality.

"In the late eighties and even more so in the early nineties, our government finally made it legal for many Chinese products to be imported into the country. Now there are so many that it seems that everything you pick up has a label on it saying, "Made in China." Also, Chinese businessmen were allowed to come into North Korea to conduct business. Even though the government did not permit our people to start their own businesses, quite a few North Koreans began buying and selling on the black market in order to survive."

Elder Cha and Esther wanted to ask more questions, but Esther knew they had all had a full day and had reached their limit. With an appropriate stretch and yawn, she said, "Gentlemen, let's call it a day and continue in the morning. Pil Soo, I can see how tired you are. Come, let me show you to your room."

As Elder Cha worked his way out of his chair to leave for his own home, he said, "You will be well cared for here in

Esther's house, Pil Soo. Tomorrow we want to hear more about your background."

Before falling asleep, Pil Soo allowed himself a few thoughts. *"Can this be real? I am being treated like a king. Will it all collapse tomorrow?"*

CHAPTER 7

QUESTIONS

On the morning of Pil Soo's last full day in the house, Esther woke up at six o'clock and began the day with prayer, her habit since she had come to know the Lord as her Savior more than thirty years earlier. Some of her most fervent prayers were for the second floor of her home, which served as a house church venue for approximately twenty believers. Now included in her daily ritual were prayers for Pil Soo.

After breakfast, Esther, Elder Cha and Pil Soo remained at the table, sipped green tea and discussed plans for the next two days. Then Esther said to Pil Soo, "We didn't hear much about your family last night. Please tell us about Myung Hee and the children."

"Gladly," Pil Soo said. "Myung Hee is the best wife a man could have, and a wonderful mother to our children—Dae Jin and Sung Yeon. Dae Jin is five years old, very active and playful like any boy his age. He loves to spend time with me and asks many questions. He's just starting kindergarten and is really bright. Sung Yeon is seven, a quiet and reserved little girl. She already helps around the house and takes good care of her brother.

"How I wish I could provide more for my children. They would be so happy if they could have cookies, candies and toys like I saw in the store yesterday. They are too young to know why they have to go hungry every day, and it breaks my heart every time they ask for more food. I have made so many promises to them that things would soon be better, but I have not been able to fulfill them. That bothers me greatly. I'm sure it bothers them, too, and they probably are already wondering if they can trust my words. I'm afraid that it is more than a little like our government leaders, who have made many promises to the people, promises that have not been kept. As a result, nobody believes them or what they say.

"I am sorry for being so negative. For the past couple days there has been so much delicious food for me, and it's not possible to stop thinking that my family has *almost nothing* to eat. Excuse me for talking like this. I am grateful for all you have done for me, and it's not right for me to dump on you like this."

Elder Cha and Esther offered quick, kind words to assure him that what he had said was not out of line. "What is in your heart needs to find a way to come out of your mouth," the elder told him. "It is important that you express yourself this way. Please go on."

"You are so understanding," Pil Soo said. "Myung Hee always has a positive outlook on life and about everyday matters. She tries hard to makes us feel loved and cared for under all circumstances.

"I met her while I was in the army. A cousin of hers was a good friend of mine in the service and he arranged for me to meet Myung Hee. We were introduced in November of 1989, and were married the following February. She was my first and only love.

"We didn't have many chances to date when I was in the army, mainly because of the terrible travel conditions where I was stationed. Also, just getting a permit to leave the base was a struggle. Yet, every time we met our feelings for each other grew stronger and stronger.

"She always tells me that I was better looking back then. That's probably because I met her while I was wearing my uniform. And I was in better physical shape from all the hard work.

"We weren't able to meet often during the three months before our wedding. I don't even remember having many opportunities to hold her hand. Our women are very proper and discrete.

"In general, they work while they are single, but not after they are married. Then they become stay-at-home wives and mothers so that they can take care of the home and raise the children. My Myung Hee was no exception.

"Before we met, she had graduated from a school with a certificate in early-childhood education. She worked for more than five years as a teacher in a nursery school for children up to the age of five.

"Do you want me to keep going?"

"Absolutely," Esther said enthusiastically. "We want to hear all about Myung Hee, your background, your lifestyle."

"Myung Hee loves working with children, and it is a

joy for her to take care of them. One thing that was hard for her—and for most of the other nursery-school teachers—was not having enough food for the children. At times, the teachers did not eat their portions in order to share with their hungry students. In our country, the demand for nursery-school teachers is high because after a baby is six months old he or she is eligible to be taken care of at a local nursery school until age five. Then they go to kindergarten for two years.

"Our women wake up around five in the morning. They start the fire, and everyone usually eats breakfast about six thirty. After the family members leave for work or school, the wife cleans the house. Then she prepares lunch. After that, she does laundry and prepares dinner. We do not have your modern appliances, so all of this takes a long time."

"Don't you ever become ill from lack of nutrition?" Esther asked.

Pil Soo smiled somewhat painfully before answering, "I'm sure it is why so many people become sick and why so many cannot recover."

Elder Cha raised his right hand to indicate that he wanted to say something. "I think you might be interested in a few statistics about this topic. The average seven-year-old boy in North Korea is five to six inches shorter and about twenty pounds lighter than boys the same age in South Korea. That's according to studies done by the United Nations. Now, Pil Soo, please carry on."

"There are other health hazards. Myung Hee once had an extremely high fever for two weeks. The doctor diagnosed it as paratyphus, which is almost always caused by contaminated food or water.

"Tuberculosis has affected five per cent of the population. There's no shortage of doctors, but we don't have enough specialists—just a few in each hospital. The biggest problem throughout the country is the lack of medicine. Even if we have capable doctors, without enough medicine they can't help people to recover. It doesn't make sense to me. As a result, people have to purchase their own medicine from the black market and bring it to the hospital.

"Paratyphus patients need several bottles of intravenous fluid in order to recover. But the government gives only one, sometimes two. The rest is the patient's responsibility. Each bottle costs about a hundred and fifty *won*. In many cases, people have to sell their belongings and even their house to buy what's needed. Some can't raise the money and that's why so many die when they become ill. My wife's cousin, the one who introduced us, died from paratyphus."

After taking a deep breath, Pil Soo explained more. "We were fortunate. Myung Hee's sister was a nurse and she gave Myung Hee several more bottles of intravenous fluid. After a few days in the hospital, the fever went down. Recovery took a couple months."

It was easy to see that Pil Soo was becoming upset about conditions back home, so when he sat back in his chair Elder Cha said, "It would be good for us to know what your plans are for the rest of your trip. We will do everything we can to help you. You may take comfort in knowing that we will provide you with some food and money for the return to your country. The money will be Chinese *yuan*, so you will need to exchange it for North Korean *won* when you are home. Convert only small amounts at a time so you won't attract attention."

Pil Soo informed them that his guides had given him

instructions about when and where they were to meet, about the return to the safe house and about the timing for crossing the river. That last item was the most critical, requiring Pil Soo and the guides to be at the Tumen River at precisely the right time to signal the guard.

"There are so many things that could go wrong," Pil Soo said. "Everything has gone perfectly so far, but can we expect this to continue? What if our expected guard is, for some reason, not on duty? If we give a flashlight signal and another guard notices..."

"Don't worry," Elder Cha said as he looked right into Pil Soo's eyes. "God will provide. We will be praying and so will members of our little congregation. Put your trust in God."

The softness of the elder's voice was comforting and reassuring. Pil Soo was grateful for what the man had said, even though he had no way of handling whatever sort of relationship he was supposed to have with God. Mustering up all the sincerity he could, Pil Soo looked at the elder and said, "Thank you for your words. They've encouraged me."

"We talked about shopping for items you can take back home, but we didn't set a time," Esther said. "It would be best to go right after lunch. I'm certain you'll enjoy the shopping. You must realize, though, that you'll be able to carry only a small amount of food across the river.

"Over the years, we've found that money is the best thing we can give to people. It doesn't take up much space and it can be used to buy what you want back in North Korea. Please don't ask where the money comes from. Just know that God will provide for you and your family."

Shortly after lunch, Esther and Pil Soo walked a few

blocks and then began shopping. He was like a kid in a candy store. In fact, he *was* in a candy store, where he picked out a variety of goodies for his children.

Later that night, Elder Cha slowly and gently introduced Pil Soo to Jesus Christ. The elder stressed that Jesus was the son of God, that he voluntarily left heaven to live on earth and that he died on the cross, bearing the sins of all people, so that they would not burdened by them throughout their lives.

"That's why anyone who believes in Jesus is guaranteed forgiveness of all sins, and an eternal life in heaven. Believing in, or accepting, Jesus as one's Savior must be done with the heart and mind. One cannot flippantly say he believes, in the hope that this will bring forgiveness and a trip to heaven. No, that's faking, that is meaningless. Such a person is not honest about his belief. A person must truly accept Jesus into his heart and fully believe that this Son of God was willing to suffer a horrible death on the cross, so that we would not have to endure a life burdened by the weight of our sins.

"That we're all sinners is true. But it doesn't mean that we are terrible men and women. Everyone sins. So everyone needs forgiveness. Jesus Christ offers it to all who open their heart to Him. This is called 'salvation,' because we're saved from our sinfulness."

From Pil Soo's expression, it was obvious that he was somewhat confused. Elder Cha knew that if he were more aggressive about sharing the Gospel message, he might well scare him off. In the past, the elder had encountered some North Koreans who had become angry when they heard the "good news" for the first time. The best he could do at that moment was to pick up a small Bible he had brought along, and give it to Pil Soo as a gift.

After good-night wishes, Pil Soo went to his room, where he looked for a place to put the Bible. To him the book appeared odd and, in a way, somewhat scary. He had never seen a book with a black cover. In North Korea, almost all books have red or orange covers.

Instead of putting down the Bible, though, he sat on the edge of the bed and began leafing through the pages. Whatever it was that Pil Soo read first, it made no sense to him, so he read another section. He did not let it bother him that all the names of people and places were foreign to him. This was a book about a different people, about a part of the world he had no knowledge of. On top of that, this Bible contained obsolete Korean spelling and grammatical patterns.

Pil Soo placed the Bible on a small table and then slowly walked around the room, deep in thought. Some of Elder Cha's words reverberated in his head. Try as he might, he could not fathom what was meant by "life in heaven." It was more than simply a new concept to him; it was more than his mind could get a grip on. In all his life he had never heard anything about sin or about someone dying on a cross or about salvation. *"If these things are so important, why have I not heard about them before?"* he wondered.

One thing he was sure of was that his vague ideas about Christianity were erroneous. Pil Soo had believed that it was in the same category with fortune telling or palm reading, of which there was an abundance in North Korea. He stopped his pacing and stood still when he recalled that while the elder spoke to him, a fleeting thought had invaded. Perhaps God was like the spirits he had heard some vague talk about years ago.

"Why is everything about this religion so baffling?" he asked himself as he again sat on the edge of the bed. *"I nodded my*

head tonight as if I understood all that Elder Cha said to me. This I did because he was trying to be so kind, and because I couldn't risk alienating a man who was so vital in my plans for returning home."

It was not nice to have such an attitude, yet what else could be done?

"It's so confusing. Kyung Jo talks to me, and I cannot understand. Elder Cha talks to me, and I am lost. Esther talks to me about how magnificent her God is, and her words mean absolutely nothing to me.

"Three of the finest people I have ever known believe in this God, in this Jesus. Can I trust that these three would not mislead me? Only because of that will I try again to figure out what they're driving at. All three have so much goodness, so much love. That makes me think there's something worthwhile about their faith.

"Esther told me two or three times each day that Jesus loves me, that God loves me and that through Him she loves me. I thought 'love' was between a husband and wife and the rest of the family. This Jesus must have been an incredible person for people to be talking about him so fervently. But they tell me He's dead. How can this be? Still it is only right, out of respect for my friends, that I pursue all of this.

"What's most important now is to give my mind and body a chance to rest in this fabulous bed. Tomorrow begins the next chapter in my grand adventure. I'll be leaving this comfortable place to start my way back home, so I must be alert to all dangers. Not a single mistake can be made."

CHAPTER 8

HEADING HOME WITH FOOD

As he showered in the morning, Pil Soo lathered up with soap and shampoo. *"What a treat this is,"* he told himself. *"And it smells so good."* North Koreans do not have body soap or shampoo, both of which are unaffordable luxuries for people like him. Instead they use harsh laundry soap.

Pil Soo was well aware that he had been doing far more thinking than usual since he began considering going to China. Thus, it was not odd that, while toweling off, his mind kept churning. On this occasion, he had a thought that had not occurred to him until then. *"Before meeting Elder Cha and Esther, my sole intention was to come to China for food and money. They've promised me both and have given me so much love, that I feel ashamed that I may be using them to achieve my selfish goals."*

He shared those thoughts with Esther and the elder at breakfast.

"There's no reason to feel ashamed," Elder Cha said.

"You're on a hazardous mission for a noble cause. Our portion in this is to be obedient to God, who has given us the means to be of service to people like you. So, no, you're not 'using' us."

As he prepared to leave, Esther handed Pil Soo a cloth bag with the candy, clothes and food from their shopping expedition. She also gave him an envelope containing Chinese money. His efforts to convey his gratitude seemed so shallow, and the more he tried to thank Esther and the elder, the more his words failed him.

Elder Cha reminded him, "When we first met, I told you that God loves you and that He has a wonderful plan for your life. And, as I told you then, I tell you now that I am praying that you will fulfill that plan. We may not know all the details concerning our journey or clearly see where the trail is leading, but God will always give us enough light to take the next step. I'm sure God will use you in a mighty way, provided you trust and obey Him. May God bless you and keep you safe as you go back to your family."

Elder Cha's firm handshake was followed by a firm bear hug from Esther, who seemingly did not want to let go. Pil Soo had never received such a memorable hug. He smiled, picked up his bag and then, as the elder held the door open, headed for the bus depot. The day before, Elder Cha had gone there with him to find out what time his bus would leave. Pil Soo deliberately arrived early for the bus, giving himself time to stop at the store and buy a few more goodies for his children.

There were two highlights for him during his three-hour ride. One was to check out the items in the bag, something that caused him to smile as he envisioned his family's reactions to the gifts. The second was to open the envelope and find out how much money he had been given. Using the utmost care, he counted the money three times to be certain he had calculated the right amount. Each counting came out to the same total. *"That's more than I earn in an entire year,"* he realized. *"I'm stunned. This money was given to me by Esther, who told me not to ask where it came from. Did it come from God?"*

Pil Soo wanted to celebrate by letting out a ceremonious shout. Or by dancing in the aisle of the bus. Or by telling people about his good fortune. But he knew he could not do any of those things, so he turned on his willpower and sat quietly.

The long ride gave him time to go through a mental checklist of what lay ahead, a process that left him satisfied that he recalled all the details. But as was his nature, positive thoughts were followed by fears. Having so much money now led him to worry about how dangerous it could be. *"If authorities searched him, how could he explain the money?"* Added to that was the concern about crossing the river with an overhead load that would be twice as heavy as before. And in that bundle would be the money. *"Elder Cha told me to pray. So do I pray that the money and I will arrive safely back home? Is that praying?"*

When the bus arrived at its destination, Pil Soo was relieved to see his companions waiting for him. Each of the guides carried a medium-sized bag containing what he assumed was food and clothing. To avoid the possibility of being overheard, they walked to a spot where they were away from everyone.

"How did it go for you?" Pil Soo inquired.

"Good," the son said. "How did you do?"

"Very well. I met these incredible people..."

The woman cut him off before he could go any further.

Then she told him, "We don't want to hear about them. It is better not to know anything about the others. If we were questioned by the authorities, knowing about another person's business could jeopardize everyone. That's why we'll never give you our names.

"But I'm glad you did well. As agreed, you must pay me one-third of your money and food. Half of that goes to my relative, the guard. That's the only way we can safely cross the river. But don't give me anything until we reach the safe house."

By the time they arrived there it was late in the afternoon, giving Pil Soo time to rest both before and after another sumptuous meal. It seemed to be an eternity before it was time to take off for the river, but once they started walking, his nervousness left. At the Tumen River they went down an embankment to wait for the moment when the flashlights would take over. After a short wait, the woman held up one hand to let the men know that the time had arrived. A blip of her flashlight was all she could afford. The three held their breath for what they felt was far too long. Then came the return signal.

To keep his belongings completely dry, Pil Soo had packed them in a waterproof bag that Esther bought for him. This was a move for which he had congratulated himself several times. Before they were halfway across the river, the three noticed something moving in the water ahead of them. A few more steps and he was able to discern the outlines of three people. It was obvious that the three saw them because they veered directly their way. Pil Soo feared that his heart would leap right out of his chest.

As the three approaching came closer and closer they

slowed down. The woman guide whispered, "Don't be afraid. Don't say anything. Just keep walking."

Pil Soo could now see that the three people approaching were women., Both threesomes ignored each another.

His feeling of relief was replaced by fears for the three women. In recent years, a stream of terrifying news had reached the ears of North Koreans, concerning the fate of refugees who had gone to China. One of the more prevalent stories was about Chinese who, after insisting that they would help North Koreans, would keep them locked up until they were able to sell them as slaves. Others would sell refugees' blood on the black market. Many North Korean women lived with Chinese men for years, sometimes in marriage, sometimes not. Although children born in such situations became citizens, the mothers lived as illegal immigrants.

Furthermore, North Koreans were being caught daily by the Chinese secret police. Most of the women sought shelter in rural areas, most of the men in cities where they had more of a chance to find employment. Those who were caught and sent back to North Korea underwent fierce interrogation and torture by government officials, for two or more weeks. Usually, the questioning was about the places they had been in China, the people they had met and any contacts they had made with Christians.

The police in both countries confiscated any money they found and all items that had information of any value, such as phone numbers, addresses and the names of people and places. For this reason, some people hid their money inside their bodies. One way was to wrap money in thin plastic and swallow it. That way, if they were searched, no money would be found. Once back home, they would discharge the plastic and the money in the bathroom.

After pulling himself out of the freezing water, dressing and paying the guides, Pil Soo waved goodbye and headed for home, where he would not arrive until late afternoon. On the way to his hometown by bus, he kept picturing the three women. *"I hope they're as lucky as I was on my trip,"* he thought. *"I could've died in North Korea without ever experiencing what China had to offer me and my family. What a fool I was for so many years."*

Somewhere amid these and a myriad of other mental gyrations, Pil Soo made a firm commitment to have a renewed passion for life and for his family. He decided he would do anything and everything to survive and provide for his loved ones. He laughed inwardly when he told himself, *"I have made my decision. Again!"*

CHAPTER 9

FOOD FOR THE FAMILY

In spite of his weariness, Pil Soo had a bounce in his step as he made his way down the dusty road toward his home. Any onlooker would have thought this man was either inebriated or had just won twenty food coupons in a card game. He had to keep reminding himself to curb his jauntiness and to not appear overly happy, for those would be clues that would cause people to suspect that something was up.

Pil Soo wanted to sneak into his house without Myung Hee seeing him, so that he could surprise her. She spoiled that idea by being right there, waiting for him. "What's cooking?" he asked with a mischievous grin, as he entered the kitchen.

"Grandma has gone for more mountain grass. Why do you have that smile on your face? Did your friend give you some food?" Myung Hee asked when she spotted the bag he was carrying.

"Yes, I have some food," he answered with a calculated

softness so that he would not blurt out with a joyous shout. "But the food is not from my friend."

Then, exactly as he had planned it while on the bus home, he slowly put one item after another on the table. Myung Hee gleefully jumped up and down. Not everything was yet out of the bag, but she knew there was enough food already for a rare stomach-filling meal for the entire family.

When she hugged him and held him tight, Myung Hee said, "What's that lovely smell on you? It's even in your hair."

"I've been to China," he admitted. "I didn't go to my friend's house as I told you. I didn't want you to worry."

She put a finger across his lips and said, "Shh. Not so loud." Both knew that government informants were in every neighborhood. As a North Korean adage put it, "Walls have ears."

Pil Soo, who saw that she was already calculating the consequences if they were found out, firmly told her, "This is something a wife shouldn't worry about." And then he began sharing with her about his trip. He showed her the money, and went on and on about Elder Cha and Esther.

"If we sell the house, we'll have enough money for Mother's noodle shop," Pil Soo said.

Then, holding up a lady's jacket he had just removed from the bag, he urged Myung Hee to try it on. It fit perfectly. She did a quick, stylish pirouette and wound up giving Pil Soo a warm embrace.

Minutes later, Grandma arrived, and five minutes after that the children popped in. Pil Soo huddled the family around the kitchen table, said he had some important news and motioned for everyone to lean forward a bit. By now all the items had been put back in the bag.

"As much as you might want to shout with joy, you'll all have to be quiet," he began softly. Next, he pulled six small packages out of his large bag. Three went to daughter Sung Yeon and then three to son Dae Jin, both of whom cautiously opened each package, stuck their faces up close and then yanked out handfuls of cookies and candies. Sung Yeon's eyes seemed to enlarge to twice their size. Dae Jin threw his head back, suppressed a howl of delight and then slapped his right hand over his mouth.

Dae Jin was the first to speak, "This is all for me? Can I eat some now?" Sung Yeon had another question, "Where did all this come from?"

"Yes, you can have some now, but only a little," Myung Hee said. "Make it last."

Giggles and smiles from his children gave Pil Soo goose bumps. It was a scene that he had choreographed so many times in his head. When the big bag was empty and the excitement had simmered down, he explained to everyone where he had been and that not a word—not a single word—was to be said to anyone about this. He knew the children would want to tell their friends about their goodies, so he reminded them three times that they could not say a word or the whole family would be in serious trouble. They assured him each time that their lips would be sealed.

During their fine meal that evening, Pil Soo leaned toward his mother and told her, "I had one meal in China where there were three meats on the table. One meat was even chicken!"

"In my many years of life, I've had chicken only at a few

wedding receptions," she responded as she shook her head in amazement.

Pil Soo said with a tinge of anger, "And you won't ever eat it again with Kim Jong-il's policies. He's destroying our country!"

"Pil Soo, don't say such things, especially out loud," Grandma scolded him. "Neighbors might hear you, and then none of us will have anything to eat. Remember, a mouse hears the whispers of the night and a bird hears the whispers of the day. There is always someone listening."

Myung Hee warned the children not to repeat what their father had just said, not to friends, not to anyone, ever.

"All right, Mother," Pil Soo went on. "Let's change the subject. Tomorrow I will put the house up for sale. If we receive even three thousand *won* for it, we'll have enough to set up your noodle shop."

Grandma gasped, and threw her hands up in joy. The children, who thought her noodle soup was the best in the world, applauded vigorously.

"This is how I dreamed it would be," Pil Soo said to one and all.

CHAPTER 10

BACK AGAIN

Within six months, Pil Soo was back in China. His reunion with Elder Cha and Esther was filled with a warmth that came from the bond between the three, a bond in which the embers of their relationship had actually burned more brightly during their time apart. Pil Soo recognized this; so he was not caught off guard during this visit when he was able to share some of his deepest thoughts, fears and hopes with these two friends. The best arrangements he could work out through the guides, he explained, allowed him to stay only overnight on this trip.

As they drank tea together on that night, Esther again asked him to provide more details about his background and his homeland.

He started off by saying, "That will be done, but first I must thank both of you for so many things. The money you provided made it possible for us to sell our home, move into town and set up my mother with a noodle-shop business she'd wanted for years. Myung Hee, my mother and the children told me to let you know how grateful they are to you. So am I.

Esther nodded graciously.

Pil Soo continued, "When I was in school and in the army, they sort of brainwashed me with socialist ideology. Everybody is fed this nonsense, but in the army it was more intense. However, for the people to survive, the North Korean society slowly became more capitalistic. Jobs were scarce, so people had to do *something* to bring in money. After I left the army, I saw many people sell their houses and possessions so they could start their own small businesses."

"I heard that the economy became worse after the death of Kim Il Sung," Esther said. "Was that true? What was your family's situation?"

"After the death of Kim Il Sung in July 1994, the government stopped giving daily food rations to the people. From 1996 through 1998, some two million men, women and children died of starvation. In the province where we live, thirty to fifty died daily in every village. Bodies of the dead were lying on the streets.

"It became so bad that a group of people, mostly men, hid in the mountains. They stole women and food from the villages.

"Much of this could be traced back to the mid-1980s when South Korea was devastated by one of the worst typhoons in its history. It did some damage in our country, but it was terrible in the south. Kim Il Sung, who had been told by some of his officials that we had enough food stored away, said he would help the South Koreans. Unfortunately, he was either deceived or the officials were inept. A tremendous amount of food was given to South Korea. And a large amount of cement was also sent to help with the rebuilding. It was only after this was done that our people realized that there was not sufficient food for us. They became upset with the 'Great Leader'. When it was discovered that we had given away too much cement and had a shortage of our own, that's when building projects had to be canceled. People lost jobs and starvation became worse. But what could they do? If Kim Il Sung said a pussycat was a tiger, then it was a tiger. He had the army and all the weapons. He promised that one day everyone would be living in mansions and eating beef soup, promises that never came true.

"We were taught to fear him. Even though many of us felt he was wrong, we didn't dare to publicly share our opinions for fear of being executed.

"On national holidays, each person used to be given two kilos of corn meal. Also, once or twice a year, people could expect one or two kilos of corn meal from their employer. If you did not work, you did not receive that food.

"In the 1980s, a working adult used to receive 650 grams of grain daily. A high school student received 550, a student in elementary school 400, a kindergarten child and a senior citizen 300. Those who contributed to the communist party or the regime received 600 grams of grain, plus sixty *won*—even after they retired. It was called 'six-sixty.' This went on until the end of the 1980s.

"In the early 1990s, people received twenty days worth of rations for each thirty-day period. In 1993 and 1994, that was reduced to fifteen days of rations per month. By 1995, a year after the death of Kim Il Sung, monthly rations were cut to five days. Some months, nothing was provided.

"The 'Great Leader' turned out to be an inept leader. It's hard to believe, but after he died, conditions became even worse. Before Kim Jong-il was president, the ordinary people lived on corn rice. It wasn't enough to satisfy our hunger, but at least we didn't have to work on empty stomachs. Right after the son came to power, he promised that he would work hard for the people. About that time, though, there was a great famine in our country. And that was followed by some of the most disastrous flooding in the history of North Korea.

"Also, Kim Jong-il invested more than ninety percent of the government's money to cover the expenses of the military-defense program. Many of the young elite poured into the Department of Defense. A steady stream of outstanding scientists worked on nuclear-weapons projects. Those things showed that the economy and the people were of no concern to the government.

"According to Kim Jong-il, we had the finest defense technology and military force in the world. But what good was that when people, even soldiers, were starving to death every day? The soldiers were so hungry that they resorted to gulping down oil designated for the maintenance of their artillery and other weapons.

"It wasn't just that there was little food. You have to understand that there are many black hands played in the food-distribution process. The government would allot food to, let's say, the First Battalion. The overall manager there would steal some for his own use. That would leave less for the First Battalion, whose food manager would also help himself. What was left for the soldiers was never enough.

"The government did nothing to help. The soldiers were told they would have to find other ways to feed themselves, so they stole from farms and looted houses. Some have robbed and killed civilians for their food. As a result, there's great hatred between civilians and soldiers throughout the country. I've even heard people say that if a war breaks out, they'll kill our soldiers before the enemy can kill them."

Esther gasped.

"During Kim Il Sung's regime, such things didn't go unnoticed. Soldiers were severely punished for committing crimes against civilians. But since Kim Jong-il has taken over, no one is protecting civilians from the soldiers. He says he doesn't need civilians, only his army. The army will protect him and his regime. This is foolish. The sons and daughters of starving civilians are the future of the armed forces. If they die of starvation, what future is there?

"Only children of high officials are allowed to study at Kim Il Sung University in Pyongyang. They also live in select neighborhoods and are totally protected from the rest of society. I'm sure they are not affected by the shortage of food the way we are."

From the pained expression on Pil Soo's face, Elder Cha could tell that it was time to change the subject. So he asked, "What type work did you do?"

"After the army, I spent five years working for the construction company that I told you about the last time. Then there were three years working for a company that installed underground sewage lines. When that ended, I started selling tofu and noodles. That did not work out, because so many people did not pay for what they took. And next was the furniture factory."

Esther expressed deep concern for Pil Soo and his family,

now that she was aware of how critical matters had become in North Korea. More than anything, she wanted to turn to a more spiritual perspective, so she said, "Pil Soo, we have prayed for you every day since your first visit."

"Thank you," he said. "I've spent quite a bit of time thinking through what you two told me last time. To be honest, most of it doesn't make sense to me. It's as if you spoke another language. Tell me, to whom do you pray? I hear the two of you say at various times that you're talking to 'the Father.' Then you say you're talking to 'Jesus, His Son.' And you counsel me to submit to the 'Holy Spirit.'"

"You remember correctly," Elder Cha said as he began an explanation of the Trinity. "It is not easy for any mind to comprehend that we have a triune God, a three-in-one God consisting of the Father, Son and Holy Spirit (who is also known as the Holy Ghost).

"Perhaps the best way to understand is to consider water. In its natural state, it's the water of oceans and the water we drink. When boiled, it turns into steam. When frozen, it becomes ice. These three forms of water become sort of a trinity of water, and it helps us see that one can be three and that three can be one."

Pil Soo, who had listened attentively, suddenly broke out in a mischievous, toothy grin. "Our regime has its own trinity: former President Kim Il Sung as father; President Kim Jong-il as the son; and official *juche* ideology as the spirit." (*Juche* can roughly be translated as "self-reliance," and promotes a philosophy that says, "Be independent. Be your own king.")

The elder and the hostess smiled at the analogy, after which Elder Cha picked up his thread of thought by adding, "God the Father sent His Son to die on the cross so that we, having been freed from the handcuffs of sin, might live to the fullest. We spoke before about the death of Jesus. It is one of numerous paradoxes that make Christianity so beautiful. Before His death and ascension into heaven, Jesus promised to send mankind a Comforter. That is another name for the Holy Spirit. Among other duties, this Comforter intercedes for us in prayer; for we are mere mortals who often struggle with the awesome power of prayer, and with what to say."

"A few pieces are falling into place, but it is still hard for me to see a picture coming into focus," Pil Soo said. "One question that keeps troubling me is, if all you say is true, then why are there no Christians in North Korea, where it would seem that your God could be of much help?"

"You'll be interested to know that in your homeland there are thousands of Christians," Esther pointed out. "As you know, they cannot openly practice their faith. That forces them 'underground,' so to speak. Unfortunately, many have been captured. It is estimated that about a third of the 200,000 people in your labor camps are Christians. Elder Cha, please tell him about Soon Ok Lee."

"This North Korean woman, who worked for the government, unjustly suffered six years of brutal treatment in prison and labor camps. After that period, she came to believe in Jesus Christ, thanks to the witness of the many prisoners who were believers. Soon Ok Lee now lives in South Korea and has written about her experiences. She writes that Christians in the camp were forced to constantly bend over and stare at the ground. They were beaten severely, especially if they looked at the sky.

"Their work was so arduous and their food allotment so poor, that their bodies shrank to little more than skin and bones. Yet while they were being beaten or were dying, those believers sang songs of praise to God as loud as they could. The Christians were given the most dangerous work, but through that and all their persecution they never denied their faith in Jesus Christ. Those are powerful testimonies to how deep the relationship develops between our Lord and us. And for that to happen, there has to be indisputable evidence of such things as the power of prayer, the love of God and Jesus, and the comfort and encouragement of the Holy Spirit."

Esther and the elder could tell that Pil Soo was stunned by what he had just heard. So they sat in silence for a few minutes.

"If I were not hearing this from you, I wouldn't believe it," Pil Soo said in an almost solemn voice. "My emotions are flying all over. The information about Christianity is powerful. The news about the sufferings is distressing, yet it is easy to believe because everyone knows that the people in prisons and camps are treated brutally. But can there be so many Christians in a non-Christian country?"

Elder Cha seemed to be waiting for that one, so he replied, "North Korea has been non-Christian only since Kim Il Sung came to power. At one time, Pyongyang was eighty per-cent Christian. It was called 'The Jerusalem of the East.' Even Kim Il Sung's own mother was reportedly a Christian.

"What is most important today is that many of your people are turning to Jesus. The church there may be hidden, but there is plenty of evidence that it is alive and strong. Young North Koreans are making frequent trips across the border. For their return home they take a bag of food, some Bibles and something for the guards. God is using those young Christians in significant ways to spread the Gospel."

"The most amazing part of all this is the number of Christians you claim are in my homeland," Pil Soo said. "I assumed that *I* am having trouble grasping many facets of your faith largely because I'm North Korean. And that led to a belief that my people simply can't understand Christianity. That so many *do* understand means that there's more thinking for me to do."

CHAPTER 11

MORE QUESTIONS

Pil Soo's third trip to China was not made until almost a year after the second. He was truly anxious to learn more about prayer, so during his two-day visit he spent as much time as possible finding out about this remarkable part of the Christian life. Elder Cha and Esther went on at length about myriad aspects of prayer, sharing and answering questions at breakfast, lunch, dinner and all times in between. For them, it was energizing to find out how receptive Pil Soo was. For him, it was fulfilling to find that his mind was more open than ever, more able to assimilate all the information he was receiving.

Elder Cha referred to something he called the five fingers of prayer. He said, "This is a guide that you can use in praying, by looking at the five fingers of your hand. The thumb is closest to your heart and it reminds you to pray for those nearest to your heart—your spouse, children, grandchildren, parents, and friends.

"The index finger, which is also called the 'pointer finger,' is a finger of authority. The Bible commands us to pray for those in authority over us: the president, legislators, state and local officials, pastors and lay leaders in the church.

"In some cultures, the middle finger is used to curse others. Jesus says that instead of cursing our enemies we need to pray for them.

"Any pianist will tell you that the fourth finger is the weakest finger on the hand. It tells us to pray for the weakest in our community and in our world. We pray for the homeless, the sick, the imprisoned, the persecuted, the addicted and the lost.

"Our pinky finger is our smallest finger and that reminds me that I am small and that I should pray for myself last of all."

It was eye-opening for Pil Soo to learn that there are so many aspects to prayer. He had regarded it as a rather simple, perhaps even simple-minded, process. But "stimulating" was the word that repeatedly came to mind as his mentors shared with him.

"Think of prayer as a telephone conversation," Esther suggested. "Place your call to God, let yourself be excited when you hear His voice and don't be in a rush to cut Him off. When we call a friend here on earth, we would not interrupt him, and we should show the same courtesy and respect to God. It's a toll-free number; so don't worry about how long the call takes.

"People sometimes say that God doesn't seem to be at the other end of the line. We all go through periods like that and, invariably, it's because many of our prayers are not being answered as we would like. I believe it's safe to say that every Christian has gone through such a 'dry' time, such a 'valley,' when God's apparent silence seems to indicate that He has abandoned us. We always learn otherwise. Thank God—both figuratively and literally!"

She and the elder pointed out that such "calls" can be made at any time, from anywhere. Having a definite time for prayer is important for some people. Most of those prefer the morning, thereby giving prayer a chance to help us focus on the hours ahead and to under gird us for what the day will bring. When Pil Soo wanted to know, "What time of day did Jesus pray?" He was informed that the Bible tells us He prayed at various times. He prayed alone (Matthew 14:23 and Mark 6:46) and He prayed with His disciples (Luke 9:28). Luke 6:12 mentions that Jesus prayed all night; and in verse 30 of chapter 24, Luke shows that He prayed before He ate. Mark recounts, in verse 35 of chapter 1 in his account, that the Lord prayed early in the morning. What appears to be more critical than when to pray is the wide range of topics that Jesus' prayers covered. There are examples of His praying to his Father about crises (John 6:15), about decisions that had to be made (Luke 6:12-15), or simply about being weary (Mark 6:31 and 46), among many other topics. "Why so much praying?" Pil Soo needed to know.

Esther replied, "As an old Christian song tells us, 'Bring everything to God in prayer.' If it's important to us, it's important to God. Those who have been in the faith for years can attest to the power of prayer. Prayer has brought about changes in the lives of many, and it has brought answers that have been stunningly beautiful evidence that God does listen and act on our behalf. It's the force behind the church. It's the reason why believers thrive even in North Korea, why they're willing to remain faithful despite punishment and death. To *not* pray is unthinkable. Among other things, that would be wasting our access to the greatest power in the universe. There's absolutely no doubt that prayer is the backbone of each individual Christian."

"Are all prayers answered with 'yes'?" Pil Soo asked.

"Not always. But trying to analyze why God does or does not answer prayers our way is beyond our limited, finite minds." Esther replied. "There've been countless instances when God's response seems to be ridiculously wrong. As time rolls by—days, weeks, even years—we learn that His answer was so correct that it staggers us. There're numerous cases when we have prayed for the sick and they've not regained their health. Why should we then bother to pray for them? Because it is the right thing to do; and because there have been so many instances of healing, including miraculous healing—the kind of healing that doctors cannot explain and that causes them to shake their head in disbelief at having been witness to the 'impossible.'"

That prompted Elder Cha to throw out a thought. "You're being told so much that it must be impossible for you to drink it all in." Pil Soo nodded and smiled, and the elder went on, "Truth is, we've only just begun. By that I mean that there's so much to prayer that we will never be able to cover everything."

"You seem to be trying to accomplish that, though," Pil Soo said with a smile that kept spreading.

"We'll soon give your mind a rest," Elder Cha told him. "First, however, just a few words about the importance of prayer, as exemplified by the life of our Lord Jesus. I've written down the appropriate Bible verses for you so that you can look them up." He handed a piece of paper to Pil Soo. "Those verses will show that Jesus believed prayer is more important than sleep (Luke 6:12), food (Matthew 4:2) or even his ministry (Luke 5:15-16). How are you ever going to have time for all your prayers? Well, simply keep in mind that Jesus Himself made time for prayer (Mark 1:35).

"Now, Pil Soo, if you can tolerate a few more words, allow me to do what we've been talking about: pray. Would you please join hands with me?" He stood up. The three of them held hands and bowed their heads. "Dear Lord, you've brought us to a special moment, a time when we pause from all else to thank you for what you've done for us, for hearing our prayers, for your grace, mercy and boundless love. We thank you for the power and comfort of the Holy Spirit; for the death of your Son on Calvary, that canceled all our sins. And now we thank you for Pil Soo, who's been exposed to your word for more than a year and who perhaps has arrived at the ultimate juncture of having to decide whether or not he can receive the Lord Jesus into his life. Grant him the discernment to deal with this."

"I've heard you use the expression 'standing on holy ground,'" Pil Soo said. "This is Esther's living room, but it feels to me that I am standing on holy ground and that God is speaking to me *right here*."

*****

"These days with you have been magnificent," Pil Soo told Esther and the elder at breakfast. "Each night, I've spent time in my room going over what you two have taught me. Last night, I did the same. There was one difference, though, and that is that I prayed at length for the first time. After that, I did more remembering. Most of all it was about how Jesus did such incredible things. 'Who else,' I thought, 'has ever turned water into wine? Who else has ever calmed a raging sea with a few words? Who else has ever healed lepers, blind men, lame people? Who else has ever raised to life a person who has been dead for three days?' Then it hit me that Jesus Himself arose from death on the third day.

"If anybody in all of history had performed *one* of those miracles, the world would stand in awe. This helped me make a decision. My decision is that I believe in the Lord Jesus, that He has taken away my sins and that I want to give my life to Him."

Elder Cha hustled to the other side of the table to wrap his arms around Pil Soo, all the while saying, "Thank you dear Lord, thank you, thank you..." While that affectionate display was going on, Esther bowed her head and offered prayers of thanks to God for Pil Soo's salvation.

Before Pil Soo left to return to North Korea, Esther gave him the usual envelope. This time, she also gave him ten copies of the Korean New Testament and ten tracts aimed at helping people understand the Christian faith and urging them to make a decision of their own.

*****

Back home, Pil Soo several times treated friends to a night of special feasting where he would always pay extra so they could enjoy some privacy. *"It's now my turn to share God's Word with others,"* he told himself before those times. He did precisely that. As he anticipated, his friends understood little of what he said, even though he tried to make everything as simple as possible. They did have sufficient interest, though, to ask questions.

"Where does God live? Over the mountains and in the sky?"

"What's heaven like?"

"Can we have *kimchee* there, every day?"

"Will Kim Jong-il be there? If so, I don't want to go there."

"You say there're millions of Christians in China and South Korea, which are now prospering. Why don't we all become Christians? Maybe then our country will become prosperous."

"How can we believe in a God from another country we know nothing about?"

"No, the biggest question is, 'How can we be talking like this? We're not permitted to talk about God, who, according to our government doesn't exist, anyway."

Pil Soo knew they were having some fun at his expense, but he was prepared for that. When such talk ceased the friends, who had been carefully selected by Pil Soo, accepted a Bible or a tract and agreed to read the material and give it serious thought. Then his friends besieged him with more questions, all about China: what he had seen, what the people were like and, most of all, what food he had eaten. They were spellbound by his recollections of the meals at the safe house and in Esther's home. But they received the biggest kick when Pil Soo told them that, "In China, even the dogs eat pork and rice."

On his way home following those evenings, he prayed for each of his friends. And he always concluded with prayers for Esther and Elder Cha. He kept thinking, *"My friends here are so skeptical, but I must recognize that this is the way I was at first. Patience. I must remember to have patience with them. And to keep praying for each and every one of my friends."*

CHAPTER 12

ON THE RUN

Kyung Jo came to Pil Soo's home one night, sat at the table with him and said solemnly, "I almost don't want to tell you this. The National Security Agency (NSA) is investigating you. They apparently have information that you've been to China."

"How did they find out?" Pil Soo asked after overcoming a momentary wave of fright. "I was so careful. Could one of my friends have betrayed me? It's horrible to think that."

"There's no way of knowing," Kyung Jo told him. "Word is out, through a friend of mine who knows about such things, that you're definitely under scrutiny."

"I'll deny that I ever went to China." Pil Soo responded quickly. "They can't prove anything. I wasn't caught going or coming, so what can they do? It's merely scare tactics. I don't want to talk to them at all, so let's skip it."

"We can't skip it. You are in real danger. We need to consider all your options and possible strategies." That is exactly what they did far into the night, while Myung Hee worked in her kitchen and listened.

Pil Soo refused to face the authorities, failing to report to the NSA after being ordered twice to do so. At first, he felt he was the one in control. Then came news from Kyung Jo that the NSA also had been tipped off that he had been talking to his friends about God. Two charges made his position far worse than just one. He was well aware that when NSA operatives interrogated suspects, they did not simply ask questions in a civilized manner. Their preferred method was to become physically abusive, brutally so. Now he had to cope with that possibility, with being legitimately terrified...with visions of a firing squad.

Two days later, a National Security agent came to the house.

"I've heard that you've been going to China," he said to Pil Soo in a gruff, no-nonsense voice.

"Who told you that? People who talk like that must be the ones who are going to China. I've never been there."

"I've done my research. You have no choice. You *must* come to the National Security office tomorrow."

After the agent left, Pil Soo walked slowly into the kitchen. He and his wife looked deep into each other's eyes. As though he had been rehearsing, he said, "Myung Hee, please prepare your best meal tonight for the whole family. Don't worry about depleting our meager supplies. And please go to the market and buy some good wine."

"But Pil Soo, that will use up the entire food budget," she

protested. He just nodded and then shuffled off.

That night they all enjoyed an uncommonly tasty meal, even Grandma, who typically ate little. When she and the children had gone to bed, Pil Soo asked Myung Hee to bring him the wine. This was going to be a memorable evening, he felt, for he was convinced it would be the last he would ever spend with his wife.

Leaning across the table and looking right into Myung Hee's eyes, he said firmly, "My decision is made. I will go to China, instead of allowing them to kill me or send me to a labor camp for the rest of my life."

Her eyes widened as she sat back in her chair and stared at Pil Soo. "I've been thinking about all of this for days, and have also made a decision. We will go together."

Now it was *his* turn to sit back in his chair. Never had he considered this possibility, but he quickly felt that this was the best solution, the one that God would be most pleased with. His mind summed it up this way. *"If we die, we die together. If we make it, we make it together."* He slowly reached across the table, took Myung Hee's hands in his and squeezed hard.

CHAPTER 13

THE OPEN DOOR

"We will have to wake up mother and the children," Pil Soo said as they started to formulate plans. "Sung Yeon can stay here with my mother; but Mother won't be able to handle both children, so it would be best to take Dae Jin to your sister's place. We need to move fast, so that this can be accomplished before sunrise. We'll pack clothes for Dae Jin in the waterproof bag, which we can then use when we cross the river. Come, let's wake up everybody, explain and say goodbye. This is not going to be easy."

Grandma understood what was going on; the children did not, so they clung tight and sobbed. It was a mile-long walk to the home of Myung Hee's sister.

"I can't believe this is happening," Pil Soo said to his sister-in-law. "We'll figure out how to get in touch with you as soon as we can."

Next came the farewells, tears, and embraces. No one

wanted to let go. Nothing, Myung Hee and Pil Soo realized, was as stingingly painful as the cries of one's child in the dark of night. The parents had to depend on wills of steel to become impervious enough to move on. Pil Soo picked up the bag and led the way to what they trusted would be freedom.

By foot they made their way to the Tumen River. There, at the takeoff spot that Pil Soo had used three times, they waited until almost midnight. This night, though, there would be no flashlight signals. All they could do was try to make it to the border on their own. He assured Myung Hee that he knew the way to the safe house, to the bus terminals and to the town where Esther and Elder Cha lived.

At long last, the moment arrived for them to slip quietly into the water. They were on the way. That alone was enough to give Pil Soo a boost of confidence.

"Halt!" That single word, screamed into the night, had a spine-chilling effect. Big flashlights were trained on Myung Hee and Pil Soo, and soon they could make out four North Korean soldiers with their rifles aimed right at them. When the two were almost out of the water, soldiers grabbed them and roughly dragged them to the embankment. What the two had feared most was happening.

They were handcuffed, shoved forcibly into a truck and transported to a military base near the border. During the next three days, both were denied food as they were questioned separately for hours at a time.

Pil Soo was usually questioned while seated on a chair, soldiers shouting in his face. Whenever his head fell forward, a guard would grab him by the hair and snap it back up, several times with such force that he fell off the chair. The guards considered that hilarious. Hundreds of times he was asked to give the names of his contacts in China and of places he had been. There was nothing clever about the process, nothing that indicated any expertise about how to deal with a prisoner. Their lone strategy was to tell Pil Soo that, if he would simply give information about relatives or friends in China, they would allow him and Myung Hee back into that country so they could come back with money—bribe money for the guards. Obtaining money, that was their *real* goal in all of this.

The worst of the guards' tactics was the assortment of ways in which they administered violence. If a punch in the face did not soften up Pil Soo, then perhaps two blows to the stomach might. Or, better yet, how about three kicks to the ribs? Blows were applied to assorted parts of the body with a heavy wooden stick that resembled a baseball bat, which was why the guards referred to this procedure as "baseball game." Blood? Nothing more than another reason for howling with laughter, especially when the blood gushed out of the nose. Pil Soo was forced to swallow his own blood. For the guards, all of this was alternately high entertainment or mounting frustration at having a detainee who refused to break.

According to North Korean law, by the way, prisoners in the custody of military personnel were not to be beaten or tortured. But since Kim Jong-il had become president, that law had been conveniently overlooked.

Meanwhile, Myung Hee was also subjected to inhuman treatment by her interrogators in another room. She was not abused to the extent Pil Soo was, but neither was she given soft treatment. At night, the two were allowed to be together in a tiny cell. Myung Hee was shocked each time, when she saw how badly her husband had been pummeled. Surprisingly, she was permitted to wash the blood off his face. Each night, when she saw Pil Soo, she burst into tears; and she wept herself to sleep. Pil Soo did not weep. His response was to become angry, and to say, "If I get out of this place alive, I'll have revenge on them for everything they're doing to me."

When it was determined that the couple would be of no useful service to the National Security Agency, the director of the prison informed them that they would be sent the next day to the headquarters prison in Pyongyang. "There, you'll rebuild ideology through high-intensity labor. This is the demand of the party."

In their cell that evening, Pil Soo whispered to Myung Hee, "Going to Pyongyang is a death sentence. Time is running out. We have to make a decision."

To his amazement, her reply was, "Yes, we must try to escape tonight." She said it with such calm.

Their cell had one high, tiny window for ventilation. It looked like the only way out—if they could figure out how to scramble up to and out of the window. But they weren't sure that their bodies could make it through that small opening.

The only other possible way out was through the door, which was made of heavy steel and was always kept locked. Each night, the guards would stand in front of the door until they sat down and fell asleep against it.

For one last time, Myung Hee and Pil Soo slowly read a message on the wall written by a former inmate:

I am suffering unfairly. I simply crossed the Tumen River
to find medicine for my sick mother and now I have to die.
The world is terribly brutal and unfair!

Pil Soo sat on his haunches in a far corner of the cell. He prayed softly, and with more passion than ever. He finished with these words: "God, if You help us escape from this prison, I will live for You and do Your will forever!"

From Myung Hee came a whispery, "Amen."

Pil Soo gave her a hug. Then they quietly did what little planning they could do for their escape. The guards, as they did each night, became louder and louder as their alcohol drinking increased. As for the prisoners, they slept until about two o'clock in the morning. The time had arrived for them to do something about making a break for freedom. Pil Soo and Myung Hee had decided earlier that the only way out was through the window. But instead, Pil Soo now obeyed a feeling that he should check the cell door. To his astonishment the door, which had been fastened with a huge lock each night, opened with just a slight nudge. There wasn't a sound from any of the guards.

Pil Soo crouched by the door, with Myung Hee close behind. He kept the door open just enough so that he could look outside to try to spot their guard. Sure enough, the guard was asleep, leaning on the door. But it was too risky to try to tiptoe around him. Pil Soo just sat still and waited. He was so tense he could hardly breathe.

About thirty minutes went by and then there came a loud yell from a guard in the nearby dining room, asking for someone to bring him a match to light his cigarette. The guard in front of the door had just waked up and rolled over, so he responded to his friend's request and headed for the dining room. This was it. This was their one chance to escape.

There was no way of knowing if other guards were awake. All that Pil Soo and Myung Hee knew was that this was the chance they had prayed about. Pil Soo opened the door a little wider, saw that none of the guards was awake, and reached his right hand back to tell Myung Hee to follow him. Both slithered out the door, which she closed behind them.

In a few seconds, they were at the rear of the building. There they realized that it was raining. They also saw that a six-foot wall stood like a mountain between them and the outside world. Pil Soo quickly devised a way to make it over the wall: He would stand on Myung Hee's shoulders, scramble to the top of the wall and then reach down to pull her up. In less than a minute they had scaled the wall.

Once on the other side, they hunched down to scan the area and determine what to do next. What came into view through the darkness could not have been more ideal: level farmland, as far as they could see. It made for easy running. They ran across the fields as fast as they could. After their nervousness subsided, they jogged, and then slowed to a fast walk. The Tumen River turned out to be less than a mile away.

At the river's edge they paused so that they could both pray for God's continued protection. And then it was into the water, their clothes overhead. After they reached the China side and had dressed, Pil Soo whispered to Myung Hee, "God has helped us escape. He has saved us." A lengthy embrace was followed by a trek to the safe house. There, the sleepy-eyed owners welcomed them inside, listened to the escape story, provided much-needed food and did everything but tuck them into bed. Later that morning the hosts fed their guests and loaned them bus money.

On the three-hour ride to the city where Elder Cha and Esther lived, Pil Soo said to Myung Hee, "You amazed me last night."

"How?"

"Your 'Amen' in the cell was the first indication that you were receptive to my words to you about the Christian faith. And your prayer before we entered the river—you prayed so beautifully. Where did all this come from?"

Myung Hee looked her husband softly in the eyes and said, "From *you*. When you spoke to me at home about your new faith, I could see that it was changing you. I also found that when I listened to your words again and again during the following days, they made sense. I had so many questions, but it was so wonderful to find out that God really exists and that there's a purpose to life. To be able to lean on Him and pray to Him has meant so much to me. You know what I mean. You've lived through the same agony as I—hearing the children cry because they were so hungry, having no money, friends dying all around us. Was that all there was supposed to be to life? If so, was it worth living just to suffer? In God there was hope for something much better. Thank you for teaching me."

Pil Soo had to grope for words before finally saying, "Don't thank me. Thank God. Thank Esther and Elder Cha. But, yes, I appreciate every word you've just said."

CHAPTER 14

THE CHILDREN

Despite all that Pil Soo had told her about Esther's home, Myung Hee was almost awestruck by what she saw there. There was a machine that washed clothes and another that dried them. A kitchen pantry was filled with more food than she had ever seen in any home. Vinyl-covered floors, small figurines of Chinese people in assorted forms of dress and a hardwood coffee table and dining room table—they all had Myung Hee oohing and aahing as Esther provided details and explanations. It was in silence, however, that Myung Hee studied family portraits on one living room wall, ones that were exquisitely framed. To herself she said, *"How much lovelier they are than the pictures we had on our wall, of Kim Il Sung and Kim Jong-il."*

As for the food Esther and her daughter served at dinner, Myung Hee had to agree with her husband's description of it as "spectacular in both quantity and flavor." She passed this on to the hostesses as part of her thanks for the grandest meal she had ever eaten. Helping to make it so was the chicken, which Esther had prepared because she knew what a treat it would be.

Myung Hee mentally agreed with another of her husband's observations. The initial feeling of uneasiness in such surroundings was virtually gone after no more then an hour, thanks to the low-key manner of Esther, her daughter and the elder.

By the time the five had gathered around the living room stove for evening tea, Myung Hee and Pil Soo had shared most of the details of their need to flee, their capture and their escape. Myung Hee now added, "When we reached the other side of the river, we talked quietly for a few minutes. We both said the same things: 'This is a miracle. He has saved us from death. We will see our children again.' On the bus here, I joined Pil Soo in making a commitment of my life to God. We will honor our vows to serve Him the rest of our lives. I felt it was important to share this so that you would know how grateful we are to God."

"It is so important for us to know that you have begun your Christian walk, and we thank you for sharing," Esther said. "While you were washing up before dinner, Elder Cha and I were discussing how similar your experience last night was, to a passage in the book of Acts. Elder Cha, would you kindly read this section?"

"Certainly," said the elder, "but in case our guests are not familiar with the account, they need to understand that this section concerns two of the most prominent Christians of that time, Paul and Silas, who were dragged before the authorities. Starting in verse twenty-two of chapter sixteen, the Scripture tells us, 'The crowd joined in the attack against Paul and Silas, and the magistrates ordered them to be stripped and beaten. After they had been severely flogged, they were thrown into prison, and the jailer was commanded to guard them carefully. Upon receiving such orders, he put them in the inner cell and fastened their feet in stocks. About midnight, Paul and Silas were praying and singing hymns to God, and the other prisoners were listening to them. Suddenly there was such a violent earthquake that the foundations of the prison were shaken. At once, all the prison doors flew open, and everybody's chains came loose.'

"The Bible goes on to tell us that Paul and Silas escaped, led the jailer and his entire family to receive Christ Jesus that very evening, and that the stunned magistrates pardoned the two former prisoners and granted them their freedom."

Pil Soo threw his head back and said, "It definitely reminds us of our miracle."

"Another biblical prison escape you might like to know about occurs four chapters earlier," Elder Cha said. Turning toward Miriam, Esther's daughter, he said, "Would you like to read us that account?"

Her response was, "I must return to my family soon, so let me synopsize." The elder nodded his approval, and Miriam said, "This story involves the Apostle Peter. He was in jail, chained between to guards. Outside his cell were more guards. Altogether, as the Bible puts it 'four squads of four soldiers each' guarded him. In the morning, he was to be put on trial, with certain death awaiting him, because King Herod had seen how pleased the Jews were when he had another apostle put to death 'with the sword.'

"The passage says that 'the church was earnestly praying'

for Peter. In the middle of the night, an angel awakened Peter, led him past all those guards and opened the iron gate leading into the city. He was a free man, thanks to prayer and God's divine intervention."

"From now on, call me 'Peter,' Pil Soo told Elder Cha and Esther. "He's the kind of man I want to be like."

Myung Hee added, "I admire Mary so much that I want to change my name to 'Maria.'" The couple had decided that, since they were changing so much on the inside due to their new faith, they should change their names, as symbols of their growing belief.

*****

Being in China was one thing; where to live while there was another. Esther graciously told Myung Hee and Pil Soo they could stay with her, and she and the elder were ever at hand with advice, consolation, prayer and much more. Esther recalled that Myung Hee enjoyed apples, so she bought some, and bananas as well. After eating most of the apples, Myung Hee hesitantly took a bite of one of the bananas. Then she took another bite, and another. Goodbye, banana. The same fate befell oranges that were given to her.

When she shopped with Esther, she was given explanations for two items that she had never heard of: feminine napkins and diapers. In North Korea, most people used cotton cloths. Toilet paper? That bordered on being a luxury there.

Retrieving the three remaining family members from North Korea was their top priority. Although Elder Cha and Esther had numerous contacts who could help, there could never be a "sure thing." One slip-up and an attempted rescue could wind up a disaster. Lives could be lost.

All of this was explained to Pil Soo and Myung Hee. They were also informed that there apparently had been a recent increase in efforts, on both sides of the border, to snare refugees. So they prayed frequently, especially the parents, who knew only too well that they were pleading with God for another miracle. They were greatly encouraged when, just one month after their own escape, news came that Pil Soo's mother and his daughter, Sung Yeon, had made it safely to China. For security reasons, they were staying with another couple somewhere in a nearby city. Other than that, details were scarce. Their son, Dae Jin, had to be left in North Korea with his aunt, because Grandma lacked the strength to shepherd two youngsters at the same time.

From the outset of their days in China, Myung Hee and Pil Soo attended services in Esther's second-floor house church. There were midweek Bible studies and prayer times, plus Sunday meetings, at which the hostess usually delivered the sermon. Most of the twenty-plus who attended were elderly. Every one of them was devout, faithful in attendance, strong in prayer and generous in tithing. The warmth and love among those people provided Pil Soo and his family with soothing encouragement. Further adding to their growth in the Christian faith were the numerous trips that he and Myung Hee made with Esther to a wide variety of other church meetings.

Along that busy trail they were introduced to a Korean church leader known simply as Pastor James. They found themselves naturally drawn to this man. Between their first and second encounters with him, they found out that Pastor James had aided refugees to escape from North Korea, and that heightened their attraction to him.

Through Elder Cha, attempts were made to bring their son, Dae Jin, to China. Each time, something went amiss. Twice, Maria's sister wasn't certain that the man who came to her could be trusted, so she refused to turn the boy over to him.

During their second meeting with Pastor James, Peter and Maria asked if he could assist in bringing their son to China. What's more, they added a new dimension by asking if he could help the entire family go to South Korea. They all were aware that the hunt for refugees in China had again intensified a notch or two, meaning that their chance of being caught had greatly increased.

Pastor James informed them that there was a good possibility that Dae Jin could be brought to China; but dreams of reaching South Korea—especially with the entire family involved—was quite likely that: a dream. "Pray earnestly," he told them. "Pray without ceasing. Pray believing. He is a God of miracles, as you well know."

Pray they did. The first of their daily prayers began each morning in the upstairs church even though, lacking heat, it was so cold that they had to bundle up.

The third time that Pastor James met with Peter and Maria, he came with news that they might be able to go to South Korea, after all. At first they were elated; but that was quickly dampened because, as Maria explained, "We appreciate all you are doing to help us, but you need to know that we won't leave our son in North Korea, even if it means that we may never be able to go to South Korea. We would rather stay in China for good, and wait for our son to cross the river."

"I can understand your feelings," said Pastor James. He reached out, took hold of their hands and then prayed passionately about the situation.

To say that those were trying times for Maria would be a vast understatement. Not only was she a mother without her child, she was a mother who knew that her son was living on a near-starvation diet in a dangerous land and with a treacherous escape attempt lying somewhere in the future. Try as she might, Maria could not overcome her anxieties. Sleep was a magical way out, but it all too often eluded her. She became ill because she felt guilty that she had so much, while Dae Jin had so little. The months without her son were dragging on: three, four, five, six.

Esther, who was keenly aware of Maria's sufferings, asked for her help in the kitchen and around the house, reasoning that this would help keep her mind off her son. She also held the sobbing Maria close to her, stroked her hair, held her hands, wiped her tears and prayed with and for her.

One morning, near the end of February, Peter was startled when Esther called to him and handed him the phone. A woman's voice he had never heard before told him that Dae Jin was safely in China. She identified herself as a North Korean and said that Elder Cha had orchestrated the mission.

Peter motioned to Maria and excitedly said, "Dae Jin is here in China."

The purported woman rescuer told Peter where she was staying and that she would call within a day or two, to make arrangements for him to pick up his son. In his mind Peter questioned the validity of the call. The best way to know for sure if this were legitimate, he decided, was to hear Dae Jin's voice; so he asked the woman to let him talk to his son. But he heard no response, despite his pleas, "Hi, Dae Jin. Are you there? Speak, Dae Jin, speak."

"I think he's afraid of the phone," the woman said. "He keeps pulling away from it. I think he recognizes your voice, but he has no idea how to respond. In a day or two, I'll call to set up a time to deliver Dae Jin to you."

After Peter hung up, he told the women about the call, hugged Maria, hugged Esther and then leaned against a wall, as if for support. There were so many questions that Peter was unable to answer. They had been warned almost daily to beware of traps, to suspect everyone who had not been approved by the elder or Esther. It was she who came up with the best way to possibly verify the caller: "She says Elder Cha sent her; let's call him to find out if he did." He did.

Sure enough, the woman called the next day and agreed to bring Dae Jin to a place near the post office in the town where Maria and Peter were staying.

"We'll be coming on a motorcycle," the woman said. "It's too dangerous to come by car, because the police check every vehicle that comes into the city. We should be there in about four hours."

Four hours later, Peter and Maria spotted Dae Jin waving at them from the motorcycle. Six months of waiting had ended. Following a joyous and tearful reunion, the four had dinner at a restaurant that specialized in barbecued food. It was there that they found out the specifics of the escape.

"Peter, it was extremely difficult for your sister to trust me," the woman began. "She knew she'd never see Dae Jin again. Word will be sent to her that he's been reunited with his parents.

"After we left her, we stayed overnight in a contact's home. We traveled all the next day and reached the river by nightfall. Some of the ice in the water was beginning to melt. I sat Dae Jin on my shoulders, where he held on to my clothes and our shoes. At the safe house in China, we gave him a bath and cut his hair so he'd look more like a Chinese boy. The owners burned his clothes so that there wouldn't be any trace of his having been there. Then they dressed him in traditional Chinese clothing."

At Dae Jin's first service in Esther's church, he was the center of attention. Grandma and Sung Yeon were there to administer hearty hugs. All the members had prayed so diligently and long, and now they were able to marvel at his presence. A seemingly endless string of thanks were offered to God for what He had accomplished. Even Grandma, who was not yet a believer, offered up praises. "Yes," she admitted, "God is amazing. It was hard to believe that Peter and Maria escaped. It was almost impossible for me to believe that Sung Yeon and I made it. Now this. God *is* amazing."

CHAPTER 15

FOOD THAT ENDURES

Life in China was unstable for Maria, Peter and the children. They were always on the alert for signs of danger—someone following them, knocks on the front door, surprise police raids that included inspections of the church. Places were assigned for them to hide when the police showed up. As much as they all were growing in the faith, continually being hunted gave them an uncomfortable edginess.

The children also wanted new names like their parents. Sung Yeon became Sharon and Dae Jin, Daniel. Sharon remained with Grandma in the home of a local couple. Keeping Daniel occupied was no small chore. He did not speak Chinese and could not risk mingling with neighborhood children, who might report him. His parents spent most of their time in the house, where they plunged into a study of the Bible. Peter used his carpentry skills to build a small, attractive offering box into which the church members could place their tithes. Among all the changes, the most memorable were excursions outside the house, when Esther would take them to church services in other cities. They heard guest speakers from Italy, Australia and other countries.

Peter and Maria also spent considerable time listening to programs on FEBC South Korea, a Christian radio station. FEBC, which has been broadcasting on the AM band into North Korea since 1973, is located on Cheju Island, south of the Korean peninsula.

Their spiritual growth was so remarkable that they were installed as a deacon and deaconess in Esther's church. That modest facility was so cold in the winter that services were conducted downstairs in the living room, where everyone basked in the heat from the stove that Peter kept well supplied with wood.

At one of those meetings, there were more refugees from North Korea than Chinese brothers and sisters. Elder Cha said to those from across the border, "Most of you came to China because you needed physical food. Such food lasts only for a short while. But there *is* food that endures. We desperately need it, because we are all part of a humanity hungry for food that lasts.

"A poet in the Bible said, 'Taste and see that the Lord is good.' Jesus Himself said, 'I am the bread of life.' He wants each of us to internalize Him. To help a bit with this process, let me teach you a new song. It is an old hymn, originally from the West.

Break Thou the bread of life, dear Lord, to me,
As Thou didst break the loaves beside the sea.

Beyond the sacred page I seek Thee, Lord;
My spirit pants for Thee, O Living Word.
Bless Thou the truth, dear Lord, to me, to me,
As Thou didst bless the bread by Galilee.
Then shall all bondage cease, all fetters fall,
And I shall find my peace, my all in all.

Afterward, the elder continued, "Please turn in your Bibles to John's Gospel, chapter six. We'll read the whole chapter together, with emphasis on verses twenty-seven, thirty-five and fifty-one."

Then Elder Cha reread his key verses: "Jesus said, 'Do not work for food that spoils, but for food that endures to eternal life, which the Son of Man will give you...I am the bread of life. He who comes to me will never go hungry, and he who believes in me will never be thirsty...I am the living bread that came down from heaven. If anyone eats of this bread, he will live forever.'

"In the beginning of this chapter, we read that Jesus miraculously fed five thousand people at one time. They were so impressed that they continued to follow Him. He knew that many were interested only in physical satisfaction. But there are other hungers; and He knew that He was the only one who could satisfy a hungry humanity.

"There is the hunger for truth, and He alone can provide this truth. There is the hunger for life, and only He can give men life and give it to them in abundance. There is the hunger for love, and He alone gives men love that outlasts sin and death. Only Jesus can satisfy the insatiable hunger of the human heart and soul.

"Jesus then claimed to be the bread of life. What did He mean? He came to Earth as a baby lying in a manger. He was born in Bethlehem, which literally means 'House of Bread.'

"But there's much more. First, bread sustains life. In that part of the world, it is comparable to our staple grain—rice. It is the essential for life. But by life I mean more than just mere existence. It is something that has spiritual meaning.

"This life is a new relationship with God—a relationship built on trust, obedience, intimacy and love. Such a relationship is possible only through Jesus Christ. Without Him, and apart from Him, we have no access to a relationship with God. We can then say that Jesus gives life. Without Jesus, we may have existence, but not life. And if Jesus gives life, then He is the essential without which real life can neither begin nor go on. But once we know Him and receive Him, all the insatiable desires of the heart and soul are fulfilled. In this sense, He is truly the bread of life.

"This passage also opens to us the stages of the Christian life. First, we *see* Jesus, then we *come* to Him and *believe* in Him. Then we *live for* Him, and ultimately we will *live with* Him. This whole process gives us life by putting us into a new and loving relationship with God. The invitation is to all men and women, but the only way to this new relationship is through Jesus. When we take God's offer through His Son, there enters a new satisfaction into our life. The hunger and thirst are gone.

"But, in our free will, we can choose to reject this offer as well. This evening, I sense there are people here who need to make a choice for Jesus and receive His food that endures. Please indicate to me if you want this true life from the one who said, 'I am the bread of life.'"

Elder Cha paused and looked around the room. One by one, a few people began nodding and then standing in positive response. With tears in his eyes, he said, "Let me pray with you." As he prayed with each one individually, the rest of the group softly sang the song.

Thou art the Bread of Life, O Lord to me,
Thy holy word the truth that saveth me,
Give me to eat and live with Thee above,
Teach me to love Thy truth, for Thou art love.
O send Thy Spirit Lord, now unto me,
That He may touch my eyes and make me see.
Show me the truth concealed within Thy word,
And in Thy book revealed I see Thee Lord.

Before continuing, the elder explained the significance of the communion they were about to partake of, pointing out that the bread and wine were symbols of the body and blood of Jesus, shed for the remission of sins.

"John's Gospel does not include the story of the Last Supper in the upper room with Jesus," Elder Cha went on. "But John's teaching in chapter six gives added meaning to the Lord's Table, to which we come again tonight. When Jesus tells us to eat His flesh and drink His blood, He is telling us to revitalize our lives with His life, until we are drenched and permeated and saturated and filled with the very life of God. So we partake of the emblems of Jesus' body and blood to identify with

His sacrifice on Calvary, and to remember His death until He comes again. And also to realize that we can be spiritually filled with His food that endures.

"The body of Christ, broken for you," he said as he passed the bread around the room. Then, as the cup of wine passed from one to another, he said, "The blood of Christ, shed for you."

*****

A month before Christmas, Esther asked Peter to cut down a pine tree. That done, she asked him to decorate it with items from a box she had stored away. Peter hung tinsel, a few lights and ribbons. Next, with advice from the women, Peter applied the finishing touches, a small ornament here, another there and—atop it all—the figure of an angel. Esther then asked Daniel to open a small box and place its contents below the tree. That was a memorable event for him, for he had been designated to put out the crèche representing the birth of Jesus.

Back in North Korea, everyone was indoctrinated with the belief that Christmas was an evil event, most likely inspired by the hated Americans. The authorities told the masses that *Jingle Bells* was a song played only in bars and discos. But Peter had always liked the song—especially the rhythm. It put him in a joyous and celebratory mood every time he heard it.

"On Christmas morning, I felt like I was a child all over again," Peter says. "It was one of the happiest days of my life. Even without a musical instrument, we worshipped and celebrated the birth of Jesus Christ. We sang the beautiful carol *Silent Night* over and over. For more than an hour, we sang. And then Esther preached a message. After the service, we had a Christmas feast with all kinds of special foods. Also, we were given our first Christmas presents."

Grandma and Sharon were also present for all that. Then they returned to the home of Esther's sister, where they had transferred for security reasons. The police search for refugees had become more intensified than ever and it was soon to lead to flights for survival.

CHAPTER 16

Hiding

One spring day Miriam, Esther's daughter, walked from her house to her mother's place, never suspecting that she was being shadowed by two members of the secret police. A minute after she entered the house, there was a loud banging on the front door. Maria and Peter had geared themselves to be ready for such an eventuality, so they hustled off a hiding place within the house.

Miriam, knowing that something was afoot, stalled so they would have time to hide. Only then did she open the door.

"Who are you and what do you want?" she asked the men in Chinese.

"We are the police and we think you're hiding refugees in this house," one of them responded. "We want you to turn them over to us."

"There are no refugees in this house," Miriam told the men forcefully.

"Isn't a North Korean woman living here?"

"No. There is nobody from North Korea here!" Now there was anger in her voice as she tried not to be bullied by the police.

"We know she's here," the other officer said. "And we know that she doesn't speak Chinese. We can prove that by just asking her a few questions. You'd better send her to the police station as soon as possible."

After another volley of threats, the men left.

A few days later, the policemen returned. They asked Peter questions, but he was unable to respond, because he did not know enough Chinese. Amazingly, they left without arresting Peter and Maria. He knew that they would come back and that they would be intent upon making arrests. It was imperative to find another place to live. But none was available.

Two weeks went by before there was another loud pounding on the door. In desperation, Esther shouted in Korean for Peter and his family to run. It was for precisely such an event that Peter had kept the kitchen window open. With his help, Maria and then Daniel made it out the window and began running. Peter hung back, concerned for Esther's well being as he heard loud shouting between her and the police. Then he recognized that she was doing this to give him time to make his getaway. He scrambled out the window. His wife and son were out of sight, even though he had used his best speed to sprint over a nearby crest. Driven by the need to find Maria and Daniel, he circled back toward the house. From behind a tree fifty yards away, he was able to tell that the police were still there. His best choice was to take a cab to the market place. Once there, he phoned a friend to find out if his wife and son had showed up. They had. To celebrate, he bought a banana and munched on it as he walked to the friend's house.

That evening, Peter called Esther to find out what had happened after he had left her house, and to let her know where he was. She told him that the police had aggressively searched the house, and were angry when they did not find anyone. And they had vowed to return.

Esther had cautioned Peter not to come back to her home until she called him, most likely a week or more down the road. But he had to go back, to pick up clothes. Refugees' filthy or worn-out clothes frequently gave them away to the police.

Making it into the house at night would not be too hard, Peter figured; so three days later he returned under the cover of darkness. He was in luck. The kitchen window was still open. In he clambered. Esther was asleep, making it a snap for him to gather up clothing, a few belongings and the Bible-study materials on which he had been working. When the trusty waterproof bag was jam-packed, Peter made his way back to his family. He phoned Esther the next morning to explain what he had done. Instead of being angry with him as he had expected, she was content just knowing that everyone was safe. At least for the moment.

Peter, Maria and Daniel needed to find another place to live since their friend, who was a church member, lived in a tiny house. It was no longer safe to stay with Esther, but she did recommend a friend who ran a brick-making factory. *"An unlikely place to go, but you never know,"* Peter thought as he legged his way there. Unlikely or not, it turned out that the owner offered him both a job and a place to stay. He was not a member of Esther's church, but his mother belonged and was a devout Christian.

Maria, too, was put to work at the factory, where she and Peter stored newly made bricks and covered them with a tarp when it rained. At times, Peter even operated some of the hydraulic machinery. Their boss-landlord paid them well at the end of each month, enabling them to pay their own way in China for the first time. The first thing they did on each payday was to set aside money they would give to God through His church. This was one of the most gratifying feelings they had ever experienced.

In all, there were fifty workers at the factory, including eight other North Korean refugees. As a result, the factory was subjected to frequent raids by the secret police. At such times, the refugees ran and hid, often behind strategically placed stacks of bricks.

When the police would come to the workers' homes, they would *always* pass by Peter and Maria's place and go to other houses first, giving the family time to scoot. Each time this happened, the two were reminded of the biblical account of the Passover that spared the lives of Jewish children in Egypt. Every Hebrew family that sprinkled its doorposts with the blood of the Passover lamb was delivered from the angel of death.

On one occasion, God's protection of Maria and Peter was so complete, that they did not know the factory and houses had been raided until the next morning. While the raid had been going on, they were blissfully watching television.

Their closest call came one day when the police swept

in quickly. Peter had just enough leeway to round up Maria and Daniel and make it to a hiding place surrounded by walls of bricks. The police were so persistent that the family had to remain there for three days and three nights. That reminded them of Jonah, who had spent a like number of days in the belly of a whale. When they emerged from hiding, each one had nothing worse than dozens of mosquito bites.

The police were becoming more forceful with each raid, and now it was time for Peter and his wife and son to create some sort of living arrangement in the warehouse. It was there that they slept for a month on thin mats placed on the concrete floor. The conditions were deplorable, but at least they were all together and they had food.

Even under these extreme circumstances they never once missed a church service, unless Esther alerted them that policemen were around. When the coast was clear, Maria, Daniel and Peter attended services every Wednesday, Friday and Sunday.

When they next saw Pastor James, he had incredible news for them. "We have almost half the money needed for your whole family to make it to South Korea. Money is being collected to cover payments to guides and drivers, as well as for trains, planes and food. Many in China and South Korea are praying for you. Whatever you do, don't say a word about this to anyone."

Three months later, Pastor James told them to be ready to leave at a moment's notice.

"When the time's right, I will notify Esther, who will give you all the directions you'll need," the pastor said. "Just tell other people that you have found another job and that you are leaving for another town.

"Peter, I've heard that your mother is not well."

"She has uterine cancer," Peter replied sadly.

"Your trip will be an endurance test across thousands of miles, including rivers, mosquito-infested areas, intense heat and much more. There's no way your mother could survive. I am sorry, but there's no choice. She must remain here in China when you leave."

A few weeks later came the call from Esther telling them where to go and when to be there.

Friends, including Esther and Elder Cha, treated the family to a farewell dinner. Embraces. Tears. Final words of parting before going to Esther's home for one last night. All of that put an exclamation mark on the night. Then it was off into the unknown for Maria, Sharon, Daniel and Peter. Well, not entirely "unknown," for what they knew most of all was that they could trust God to be with them. Little could they imagine how much they would come to rely on Him during their journey.

CHAPTER 17

GUIDES AND DIVINE GUIDANCE

In the morning, Peter and his family, accompanied by Esther and Miriam, went to the railway station. There they met Pastor James and the guide for the first leg of their trip to South Korea. Saying farewell to Elder Cha and Peter's mother last evening had been difficult. Saying farewell to Esther that morning was another bittersweet time, when no one wanted to let go of the last hugs they would ever share with her.

Then excitement rose as Peter, Maria, Sharon, Daniel and the guide boarded a train that would take them far away to Kunming, the city of eternal spring, in the southwest part of China. For them, the trip seemed eternal. In reality it was a weeklong junket, marked by lengthy layovers in railway stations as they awaited connecting trains.

In Kunming, another guide took charge and they stayed overnight in his home. Next came an all-day, all-night bus ride that left everyone bone weary and unprepared for the first fright of the journey. It came at a seeming border crossing that proved to be only a provincial checkpoint.

"When it's our turn, should I look at the guard?" Peter wondered. *"What if he asks me a question? How could this be happening without any warning from our guide? Why didn't he tell us?"* It was only then that he remembered that their Chinese guide did not speak any Korean. When he mentioned this to Maria, they both laughed out loud.

The laughter subsided in a flash when a stern-looking guard approached their group. He asked a few questions of the guide but, to everyone's relief, let them pass through.

And then the truly adventurous part of the ordeal began. Their two new Chinese guides spoke no Korean, so all communication had to be done via gestures and hand signals. The guides had arrived at the designated meeting place with only one motorcycle, so they had to take off and come back with a second one. Peter and Daniel sat behind the driver of one motorcycle. Maria and Sharon did the same on the other bike.

A thirty-minute ride brought them to the house of one of the guides, where they were instructed to change their clothes and put on long-sleeved shirts and long pants. That did not make sense to Peter, now that they were in what seemed to be a semi-tropical area.

Another ride, this one two-and-a-half-hours in the hot sun, ended with signals for everyone to start walking along a jungle-like path. The guides did their best to communicate with Peter. They let him know that within half an hour they would be at the Laotian border, where border guards patrolled the river in boats. Or at least that's what he thought they meant.

Peter's interpretation of the sign language was really quite good, except that the arduous trek to the river took almost four hours across hills and valleys, and through thorn-infested bushes that snagged everyone's arms and legs. If nothing else, at least they now knew why they had changed clothes.

To add to the misery, the guides slowly realized that they were lost in this wilderness. They admitted it to Peter, and indicated that the family should wait while they went on their own to find the river. But there was one further problem: almost all their food and water had been consumed. When Peter studied the rugged mountains above them and the dense jungle ahead, he thought, *"We can't survive long in here. Lord, we really need your guiding hand."*

His next thought was about stories of how unsuspecting people were sold as slaves to poppy farmers in this golden triangle region between Vietnam, Laos, Thailand, Burma and China. He knew that he could not dwell on that, so he told his family, "Let's pray and ask God to help us." The four held hands and prayed fervently.

Evening was rushing on. Still no word from the guides. The children huddled beside Maria and Peter. Then, finally, came the best sound of all: a call from one of the guides. They followed his voice until they all were together again. Another thirty minutes and they were close to the river, at a hut made out of tropical leaves. There they slept fitfully.

Sharon, who had attended a Chinese school for a year while staying with Esther's sister, told her folks that she felt she might be able to talk with the guides. Her knowledge of the language was far better than Maria and Peter had expected, so Sharon was put in charge of communicating.

After her first such effort, she told her parents that they

were at the Mekong River and that a big boat would be coming to pick them up. But no boat came. The guides brought some water and they sat around and finished the last of their provisions—a few cookies. Mosquitoes kept up their dive-bombing attacks. Peter told his family, "We were able to survive on almost nothing back in North Korea, so we can surely endure tonight and whatever lies ahead, as long as we cling to the Lord."

An almost steady parade of boats and barges went by the next morning, as the group watched from behind riverbank bushes beside the mighty Mekong. This river meanders through Yunnan Province in southern China, and forms the border between Myanmar (formerly known as Burma) and Laos. It also forms most of the border between Laos and Thailand, and flows across Cambodia and southern Vietnam before reaching the South China Sea.

It was not until four in the afternoon that the guides sighted their large rescue boat. They were stunned when the vessel went right past them and into a small cove. But they soon realized that was done to move out of the sight of an approaching larger coastguard vessel carrying the flags of all five surrounding nations. Half an hour later, the motorboat pulled up at the pier just below the group. Just then, about a quarter mile upriver, they saw the coastguard obviously pursing them. Amid urgent yells from those on the rescue boat, the family quickly clambered onboard. They held on tightly as the pilot gunned the engine and swiftly pulled away from the approaching coastguard vessel.

It was not a smooth ride. The boat, which was not in good repair, took a pounding from the unusually rough water. It was impossible to communicate with the sailors, who were

Laotians. The family members were hungry. It had been almost two days since they had any substantial food to eat. It was also getting late, and everyone was exhausted.

One of the guides asked Peter if he had seen their cell phone. It was passed from one guide to another in case of emergency, and now seemed to be lost. The guide had to make a phone call, so they stopped along the shore. Peter knew this was not in the plan, but he did not have any other choice than to go with the flow.

At nightfall, the guides came back with some food and water. There was a bag of "sticky rice," a delicacy in the region, as well as some canned goods, but no spoons or forks. It all looked very unusual, but Peter and his family were too hungry to even consider what they were eating. They devoured the food using their bare hands.

They spent that night in the jungles of Laos. Mosquitoes were constantly biting them. It was the longest night they had ever known, and all they wished for was the daylight.

The next morning their faces were swollen because of the many mosquito bites. Peter commented laughingly, "We look like lepers!"

It was about eight in the morning when the guides came back after trying to make some phone calls. They indicated to Peter that the phone calls did not go through. So the whole group traveled two more hours into the jungle, to make one more attempt to call their contacts. By then, Peter was extremely nervous, again not knowing what was happening. But once they approached the Thailand border, two Korean-speaking men came to meet them. One of them was a church elder. Peter was so relieved to be able to communicate after days of confusion and frustration.

This was an area well known for its notorious Thai border guards. It appeared obvious that this crossing could turn disastrous. Instead, the inexplicable happened. There were no guards at the crossing point. Everything went so smoothly that there was time for the two men to treat Peter and his family to a fine breakfast and a leisurely tour of a nearby city.

Then brand-new passports were handed to Peter, one for each member of his family, and they headed toward the airport. At two in the afternoon, the family boarded a plane bound for Bangkok. It was a relatively small aircraft, but Peter was very excited to fly for the first time in his life, something he had wanted to do since he was a little boy. As the plane took off, he felt free already. Enjoying this sensation of freedom in flying through the air took his mind off everything else.

In Bangkok, they were taken to a safe house for North Korean refugees. There it was decided that it would be best for Peter's family to go to the Cambodian safe house. So in the morning they packed up again and started east toward the Cambodian border by car. They spent the night near the border, and the next morning the younger guide paid a Thai farmer to transfer the children to the other side in his wagon. Peter and Maria crossed the border carrying a camera and luggage as though they were tourists.

Reuniting on the Cambodian side of the border, they took a taxi for about four hours and arrived at a Cambodian tourist town near the ocean. There the elder approached Peter and Maria and fully explained their situation.

"I didn't tell you earlier because I didn't want to discourage you. There were too many North Korean refugees in Bangkok. It would've taken much more than six months waiting period before you could travel to South Korea. However, by tomorrow you'll arrive at the Cambodian safe house and the wait will be shorter. You are truly safe now, so have a good rest tonight. God bless you."

Maria and Peter simultaneously said, "He already has!"

CHAPTER 18

UP, UP AND AWAY

The next morning after a good breakfast, the family boarded another boat that traveled up the river to Phnom Penh, the capital of Cambodia. There they took a taxi to the district where the foreign embassies were located. Just a few minutes after the elder's call to the South Korean embassy, a car arrived and took the family to the safe house located in a church building.

In the safe house were twenty-eight refugees from North Korea, one of whom was a woman from Peter's hometown. She had left a year later than Peter and he was anxious to hear more current news from home. Then he, Maria and the children were shown to their room, a bonus they didn't fully appreciate until a few days later, when they learned that their family was the only one that had a room all to themselves. Most of the people there had left their families behind, so at the safe house men and women were separated, with roughly seven people in each room.

Strict rules had to be followed. It was no problem for all residents to participate in preparing meals and cleaning up. The difficult adjustment was that they could not step outside the church property. Cambodia had diplomatic relations with North Korea, which meant that refugees, if caught, would be sent back home.

Newcomers were generally reluctant to say much to the others for the first few days, after which they opened up and engaged in conversations. Soon they all appreciated one another's plight, came to trust each other and developed a genuine camaraderie. Peter determined that about sixty percent of the people had come there with the assistance of Christian groups, twenty percent had received help from businessmen and the rest came on their own. Many of their tales of how they endured were stunning, which worked wonders in the bonding process.

As the sapping summer heat and humidity drained one and all, more and more people ventured to the backyard to exercise a little, to chat and to breathe fresh air. One of the nicest aspects of being there was that not only were Maria and Peter close to the church, they were *in* it and enjoyed attending two services there every day. Many of their comrades came to know Jesus as their Savior, another factor that solidified their relationships. But some, who all their lives had been told that Christianity was evil, found it impossible for their minds to think otherwise.

What North Koreans want more than anything else is freedom—freedom to attend meetings promoted by the regime and freedom not to attend, freedom to express themselves and freedom to be silent. Peter couldn't refrain from sharing a thought with Maria. "Those who have enjoyed freedom should perhaps seriously ponder what it must be like for those who are not so blessed."

Life in the church had its drawbacks, including negative rumors that seemed to emerge from the woodwork. One was that North Koreans were no longer able to enter South Korea. Another was that, for reasons not explained, "everything" was becoming worse since September 11, 2001. Living in tight quarters also took its toll. Most of the time, though, the people learned to share and to trust each other.

Best of all, they were blessed to have two pastors—a husband and wife—who were deeply dedicated to their ministry for Christ. Furthermore, the two were medical doctors who were able to care for the refugees.

Loosely structured rules were used to determine the order in which people were selected to go to South Korea. Usually, seniors and pregnant women were given top priority, followed by the families with the most children. Careful records were kept and every effort was made not to detain anyone for more than three months.

Whoever received brand-new clothes and shoes from the pastors was assured that he, she or they would be departing within a week. In what may have been a clever ploy to attract folks to the morning church service, news about who would be heading for South Korea was always announced at that time.

Waiting day after day, week after week, had a dulling, numbing effect. Maintaining an upbeat attitude, though, was not all that difficult for those at the church, perhaps because each person had won battles against even more challenging situations to arrive at this moment.

The morning they were notified, the family could not

believe it was finally happening. Peter was mindful of those who stayed behind and had to wait for their turn so he could not fully express himself publicly. Yet in his heart, he was very emotional and overjoyed. He was so grateful to God and tears of happiness flooded his eyes.

There were many Koreans from the North and the South at the airport. The family had to be on the alert the whole time. They were extra cautious because of an incident that had taken place at the airport, just a couple of months earlier: North Korean officials captured another family that was leaving from the safe house. Later, the pastor miraculously rescued them.

As the family finally boarded the jet plane that would take them to Seoul, Peter was amazed at the size of the aircraft. He had never seen a commercial airliner this size. Everything on the plane was so clean and modern, and he felt very proud of the South Korean jet on which he was a passenger that day.

Once on the aircraft, they were monitored closely for security reasons. In the past, North Korean spies or Korean-Chinese who disguised themselves as North Korean refugees escaped once they arrived at the Seoul airport.

The flight attendants on the airplane were very kind to them since they all knew that Peter and his family were refugees. The family was seated in the back and protected and cared for by the crew. When the captain made his final announcement about landing, again tears flowed freely down both Peter and Maria's cheeks. This was a dream come true. Nothing could have emotionally prepared them for such a time as this.

As the plane taxied to the gate, Peter recalled all they

had experienced to reach this very moment. He remembered how they crossed many rivers and mountains. How they were arrested and tortured because of their quest for freedom. How he had to be separated from his son and daughter. The days they had to go without any water and food. The nights they had to spend in the tropical jungles. But now those hardships seemed so worthwhile!

Even the air they breathed felt different. When the family saw the Inchon International Airport in Seoul, they were flabbergasted at how enormous, modern, spotless and shiny the buildings were. Even the biggest and the best building in Pyongyang, North Korea could not be compared with this airport. There was such a wide assortment of flowers that they all had to touch some of them to find out if they were real. They were.

The family was taken to a private room. Their entry was not a public affair. Just a few government officials greeted them and took a picture of the whole family. They also asked Peter and Maria to share a few thoughts and feelings about landing in Seoul. After that, they were taken outside and transported to a government office to be questioned and investigated regarding their arrival in South Korea. They had to go through the regular entry process directed by the South Korean government.

As they traveled through the streets of Seoul, they were even more amazed. Everything they saw looked modern, advanced, bright and clean. In North Korea the buildings had to be uniform and controlled but here in South Korea, even the houses seemed to have individual freedom and personality. Peter felt free just looking at the different houses and buildings, and how they were laid out in relation to each other. He wanted to visit every house and see how each family lived inside the buildings.

Peter and his family again thanked God for all the miracles He had performed throughout their journey. Indeed, God had orchestrated their exodus, as well as their arrival in the promised land.

CHAPTER 19

LIFE IN FREEDOM

What lay ahead, however, seemed almost surreal. For a month the family was housed in a government building, where Maria and Peter were interrogated, in most cases separately. They were questioned about everything, including the name of the kindergarten school they attended, the classes they took in elementary school, the school songs they sang and hundreds of other items. Officials wanted details about trips to China, their capture, breakout and the escape route to South Korea.

In the evenings while comparing their days, the two discovered they had given interviewers conflicting answers to some questions, with Maria having a frustrating time when asked for dates of various events. Still, they knew that there was a purpose to all this, namely, to sort out those people who were not true refugees from North Korea. What the officials wanted to accomplish, more than anything, was to ferret out Korean-Chinese who sought entry into their country.

Security was very tight. Not only did they need permission to go to the bathroom, they were accompanied at those times by an armed guard. Following extensive medical check-ups, the family was transferred to a halfway house. The days there were more pleasant, especially when they were given lengthy tours of Seoul—everything from tourist attractions to department stores and shopping malls. On these trips, there were the ever-present guards, who by then almost seemed to have been grafted to the bodies of the family members. Thankfully, they were not overbearing and, in fact, got a kick out of the excursions and the family's spontaneous and joyous responses to a world they never knew existed.

Wherever Peter, Maria, Daniel and Sharon looked they seemed to spot something else that blew them away. Cars, cars, cars. Tall, tall, tall buildings. Clean streets. People laughing. Stores filled with more clothes, toys, furniture and electronic equipment than they had ever seen. These and other things they noticed kept them talking excitedly far into the nights.

What impressed them the most? The food. Their taste buds may well never forget their first hamburgers. Or their first pizzas. Restaurants and snack bars were never more than a few paces away, or at least that was the image that stuck in their minds. However, each time they ate, Peter could not stop thinking about his relatives and friends who were starving back in North Korea. He deeply wished that he could send food to them. He knew that was not possible, but he longed for the day when North and South would be reunited once again. He was sure that when that happened there would not be a single starving person on the Korean peninsula.

Other thoughts and feelings had to be dealt with too;

primarily resentment about how the North Korean propaganda machine had poisoned an entire nation with lies about how horrible life was elsewhere. Only now could they evaluate and find that their homeland was the one that was blighted, that their people were the ones who were being deceived at every turn and that Kim Jong-il ranked among the cruelest men in world history. Admitting this to themselves was painful in myriad ways and long-into-the-night talks were invariably tearful. Peter and Maria wished that they could somehow let fellow North Koreans know the truth. They had heard that the truth "sets men free," but they had experienced the opposite, for it was their newfound freedom that was letting them see the truth.

There was just one cloud that hung over their life in Seoul. Well, actually it wasn't a "cloud." It was that some sections of the city had significant air pollution because of the fumes from all the motor vehicles. Knowing that, and knowing that they would soon be sent to an apartment that would be their government-subsidized home for at least a year, Peter prayed specifically that they would not wind up in one of the polluted areas.

A random number, drawn by each person or family from a small box, determined who was assigned which apartment. The next day, all those in the latest batch of refugees were taken to their units. It was February 6, 2002, a day imbedded in the memory of all the family, for that was when they took possession of a beautifully furnished two-bedroom unit. What's more, it was in a lovely residential section of Seoul where there was little traffic—or pollution. No matter how often they said it to each other, none of the four became upset with their favorite expression, "Is this really ours?"

Well, yes and no. North Koreans seeking asylum in the south were allowed to stay in their apartment for one year, rent-free. During that period, the government even paid them a minimum salary. At the end of a year, they would be on their own.

The next month was abuzz with all sorts of activities: memorizing the names of the streets in their neighborhood; finding out where to shop for food and clothes; arranging for the children's schooling; finding time to drop in for a hamburger one day and a milk shake the next. Peter obtained a driver's license in the event that he might need it in the future.

Skills had to be sharpened, so Maria and Peter signed up for morning classes that would prepare them to join the local work force. Maria's goal is to become a professional seamstress for a company that specializes in clothing alterations, or to land a job in the fashion field. She chose that profession because one of her sisters is a professional seamstress and pattern maker. A more long-range goal is to save enough money so that she can assist her family back home when that wondrous day arrives on which the two Koreas are reunited.

Morning sessions for Peter consist of training in interior design, construction and carpentry. Evenings are spent learning how to use a computer, with most of the emphasis on developing skills that can be utilized for interior-design work.

He also recognizes the need of Christian fellowship and friendship. Peter's family was introduced to a good church where the whole congregation welcomed them with open arms. They are constantly helping and providing support for them. And there are other North Korean families who attend the same church. A weekly discipleship meeting and fellowship time is held just for North Korean families. Every Sunday after the service, all the North Korean families get together for a time of Bible study and fellowship. After the fellowship, they have a recreational time where they play games, learn new songs and enjoy each other's company. This is their time to connect with each other and share the latest news. It is also a time to recommit themselves to God and to His purposes.

After reflecting on the experiences of his life in North Korea—the trips for food, getting caught at the border, the escape, life in China, the exodus, resettlement—Peter can boldly say that all he needs is God. He often expresses his feelings to Maria, "I'd rather live in North Korea as a Christian than live here in South Korea as a godless millionaire." They cannot imagine their lives without God and His love. Their growing passion is to be able to someday soon share this faith with their friends in North Korea.

Like Soon Ok Lee who spent six years in North Korea's prison camps, Peter often shares publicly about the situation of North Korea. He too believes, "...if we pray to God and follow His assistance, we can bring the gospel into North Korea. Many of the people there are hungry and dying, but...it is more important to send the Scriptures than to send rice."[1]

For the family, each day begins at five in the morning and is set in motion by a prayer time. It is a ritual Peter has abided by, throughout his days in China and in all places where he has lived since then. Thank you, Esther.

---

[1] Soon Ok Lee, *Eyes of the Tailless Animals,* Bartlesville, OK: Living Sacrifice Book Company, 1999, p. 154

CHAPTER 20

TODAY, TOMORROW AND BEYOND

Peter turned out to be somewhat of a visionary. Or so it would appear. His fanciful peering around the corners of time and space, though, may not be so unrealistic. After all, God had granted an unusual number of explicit answers concerning earlier visionary matters. One not mentioned before concerns the size of the church in Esther's home, where a typical turnout was twenty people. Most such house churches have congregations of between twenty and thirty members, but Peter made a concerted prayer effort for Esther's group to grow to fifty regulars. As preposterous as that seemed, by the time he left China after eighteen months there, Esther's church had fifty-three solid members.

By earthly standards, Peter is not well educated. Let us not forget, however, that there are other standards by which men can be judged. When it comes to applying one's faith to the rigors of life, Peter must surely be a graduate student. His story, though, is not his own. Without Esther and Elder Cha, without Pastor James and others in the ministry, and certainly without God's frequent intervention, there would not be a story. If Peter's visionary posture is to be translated into a succession of realities, there will have to be more Esthers, more Elder Chas, more pastors, more Godly touches.

What are Peter's apparently unrealistic visions? Let's take a look at them.

To begin with, he has longed for several years to enter a full-time ministry for the Lord. What's so visionary about that? Well, a Christian pastor, one who regularly came to the halfway house where Peter stayed in Seoul, felt that it was an unwise choice. In his words, "When North Korean refugees come to South Korea, many make a hasty decision about going to seminary to become a pastor. This is a move that should not be made out of simple gratitude to God, but with prayer and careful consideration. You should be sure of God's calling before even considering seminary. Just one of the questions to be dealt with is, 'Where are the funds going to come from to pay for the schooling and to take care of the family?'"

In light of that pastor's advice about not entering the ministry, Peter reconsidered and decided, *"I may not be able to preach or become a pastor, but I can and will serve in any capacity that God enables me to handle."*

He has reconciled himself to that, largely because he is motivated most of all by another visionary prospect. "My vision is to build a church in my hometown so that I can invite everyone to come and receive all that God has for them. In my head are the plans for the roads that will wind their way to this church. I also know exactly where that church will be built—on a hill next to a beautiful park.

"None of this can happen until North and South Korea reunite. Many feel this is never going to happen. I disagree. Already there are good signs, and Kim Jong-il is aging and has heart disease and diabetes. As cruel as he has been, we need to follow the teaching of Jesus to forgive him and pray for his salvation. The masses are starving for food, starving for freedom and starving to be allowed to openly love and worship God. There are vast differences between the North and the South, but none so great that a united people—God's people—cannot conquer by persevering and praying."

Topping it all off are the visions of the other family members. Sharon wants to be a teacher so that she can share God's love with the children of North Korea. Daniel's prayer is that God will enable him to become a pastor. As for Maria, she is prepared to stand by her husband, knowing that he will always need a faithful helpmate, both at home and in whatever form of ministry the Lord has for him.

What started out being all about food has become all about God.

ACTION STEPS

North Korea, "the Hermit Kingdom," with just over twenty million people, is one of the world's most reclusive and secretive nations. This makes it difficult to obtain accurate information. But one thing is certain. A very large number of Christians there are severely persecuted, often to the point of death. In fact, it is estimated to be the worst nation in the world for the overt persecution of Christians.

Under the influence of this pressure, North Korean people are obviously not publicly open about their faith. It is therefore very difficult to know exactly how many North Korean Christians there are. An underground Church does flourish in the northern areas, but is strictly organized around family lines. The house churches meet in secret. Sometimes up to eighty people come together in caves in rural areas. From the beginning, Christian basics are also taught to the children. At a later stage, the young adults try to find Christian partners, even if this means a social sacrifice.

In 1996, Open Doors started active ministry to persecuted Christians in North Korea. We support and encourage them by delivering Bibles, food, medicine, radios that can receive FEBC, bicycles, and leadership training. We also support key workers in China, like Esther Li and Elder Cha who have dedicated their lives to help Korean refugees.

There are widely divergent and sometimes conflicting reports from those who visit North Korea and especially from those who work among North Korean refugees. For example:

- The reported number of people who have died of starvation in North Korea since 1995 varies from one million to five million.

- The reported number of Christians in prisons or labor camps in North Korea varies from fifty thousand to seventy thousand.

- The reported number of North Koreans who have crossed the river to Northeast China in the past decade varies from three hundred thousand to two million.

- The reported number of North Korean refugees who live in China varies from fifty thousand to three hundred thousand. Up to fifty percent of them are reportedly Christians.

- The reported number of Christians in North Korea varies from ten thousand to five hundred thousand.

There is no doubt that the North Korean refugee problem is a serious one. China labels them illegal "economic migrants" and not refugees. The Chinese employ bounty hunters who actively seek out refugees for deportation, which results in certain imprisonment or death by starvation, disease or torture.

Two South Korean pastors and two laymen were recently imprisoned in China because of their pastoral and humanitarian work among North Korean refugees. They await court decisions on their fate.

North Korea is currently cracking down on border guards who close one eye or take bribes. South Korea allows only a very limited number of North Korean refugees like Peter and Maria into the country annually.

Criticized by humanitarian organizations for failing to aid North Koreans who flee famine and oppression to China, the office of the United Nations High Commissioner for Refugees has promised to take steps to stop their forced repatriation to North Korea; but to the date of this writing, nothing much has changed.

Christian organizations are hard at work in the region to help these refugees in every way possible. South Korean, Japanese and Chinese Christians risk their own freedom to provide the refugees with humanitarian aid and teach them about the Christian faith. It is difficult to share much about their work without creating a security problem for them. But the situation of these refugees needs our immediate attention. Here are some things you can do:

- First, become as informed as possible about the conditions of North Korean refugees (see Suggested Reading and Viewing pages).

- Contact your government representatives regarding assistance from your country.

- Arrange and/or attend prayer vigils or prayer meetings for North Korean refugees and Chinese Christians who are aiding them.

- Join a "prayer walk" tour visiting North Korea. Contact the Open Doors office in your country for more information.

- Financially support ministries working among North Korean refugees, including Christian broadcasters like FEBC.

- Tell others about the situation, need and opportunities.

The least you can do is the most you can do.

Pray!

Here are fifteen suggested prayer requests to assist you:

- Pray that the Lord will give strength and courage for believers to remain faithful and develop safe methods for communicating with one another.

- Pray for Christians to stand firm against the statewide idolatry of the nation's leadership.

- Pray for Christians and their families incarcerated and worked to death in violent prison camps.

- Pray that God will give His grace to brothers and sisters undergoing brutal torture or facing execution for their faith.

- Pray that Christians who are tortured to the point of death will not reveal the identity of the others.

- Pray that foreign aid will reach North Korea's starving population.

- Pray that many North Korean Christians will become teachers to spread the Gospel, so that society will change from within.

- Pray for wisdom and discernment for those who minister in China to North Korean refugees.

- Pray for Christian missionaries imprisoned in China for helping North Koreans.

- Pray for North Korean refugees in danger in China.

- Pray for unhindered delivery of the word of God into North Korea.

- Pray that many North Koreans will recognize the Lord Jesus as the only Way, Truth and Life.

- Pray for good health for our Christian co-workers in the area.

- Pray for the elderly and infirmed, who have continual needs for medicines and medical care.

- Pray for the practical needs of Christians living in the remote areas. They go to the mountains to have secret worship meetings; therefore, they need flashlights to shine in the darkness of the night. Pray that their lives will also be "flashlights."

RECOMMENDED READING

Belke, Thomas J. *Juche: A Christian Study of North Korea's State Religion.* Bartlesville, OK: Living Sacrifice Book Company, 1999.

Hawk, David. *The Hidden Gulag: Exposing North Korea's Prison Camps.* US Committee for Human Rights in North Korea, 2003.

Kang, Chol-Hwan and Rigoulot, Pierre. *Aquariums of Pyongyang: Ten Years in the North Korean Gulag.* New York: Basic Books, 2002.

Kim, Hyun Hee. *The Tears of My Soul.* New York: William Morrow Co., 1993.

Lee, Soon Ok. *Eyes Of The Tailless Animals: Prison Memoirs of a North Korean Woman.* Bartlesville, OK: Living Sacrifice Book Company, 1999.

Natsios, Andrew. S. *The Great North Korean Famine: Famine, Politics and Foreign Policy.* Washington, DC: U.S. Institute of Peace Press, 2002.

Vollertsen, Norbert. *Inside North Korea: Diary of a Mad Place.* San Francisco, CA: Encounter Books, 2004.

Werner, David. *Where There Is No Doctor: a village health care handbook.* Palo Alto, CA: The Hesperian Foundation, 1977.

Human Rights Watch (HRW) Report. *The Invisible Exodus: North Koreans in the People's Republic of China.* November 2002, Volume 14 #8.

31 Days Of Prayer: North Korea. Singapore: OMF International, www.omf. org, 2004.

RECOMMENDED WEB SITES

http://www.hrw.org/reports/2002/northkorea/norkor1102.pdf

http://www.nkhumanrights.or.kr

http://www.web.amnesty.org

http://www.hrnk.org/hiddengulag/pdf/Overview.pdf

http://www.kimsoft.com/2000/jucheNK.htm

http://www.chosunjournal.com/index.html

http://news.bbc.co.uk/1/hi/programmes/this_world/3436701.stm

http://www.SeoulTrain.com

RECOMMENDED VIEWING

Chol, Anh. "Children of a Secret State." A **Channel 4 UK film broadcast in many countries (See www.bekkoame. ne.jp/ro/renk/ahnchol/ahnchol_e.htm).**

"North Korea: More Love To Thee." Video produced by Voice of the Martyrs, P.O. Box 443, Bartlesville, OK, USA.

"North Korea: Suffering in the Secret State." Video produced by Christian Solidarity Worldwide, UK.

"Seoul Train." Video produced by Lisa Sleeth and Jim Butterworth. Incite Productions, 2006 (See www.SeoulTrain. com).

FOR MORE INFORMATION ON OPEN DOORS

For updated prayer points, or to learn about additional resources and involvement opportunities with the Persecuted Church, please contact the closest Open Doors office:

Open Doors
PO Box 53
Seaforth
New South Wales 2092
AUSTRALIA
www.opendoors.org.au

Missao Portas Abertas
Rua do Estilo Barroco, 633
Chacara Santo Antonio
04709-011 - Sao Paulo, SP
BRAZIL
www.portasabertas.org.br

Open Doors
30-5155 Spectrum Way
Mississauga, ON
L4W 5A1
CANADA
www.opendoorsca.org

Åbne Døre
PO Box 1062
DK-7500 Holstebro
DENMARK
www.forfulgt.dk

Portes Ouvertes
BP 139
F-67833 Tanneries
Cedex (Strasbourg)
FRANCE
www.portesouvertes.fr

Offene Grenzen Deutschland
Postfach 1142
DE-65761 Kelkheim
GERMANY
www.opendoors-de.org

Porte Aperte
CP45
37063 Isola Della Scala, VR
ITALY
www.porteaperteitalia.org

Open Doors
Hyerim Presbyterian Church
Street No. 403
Sungne 3-dong
Kandong-gu #134-033
Seoul
KOREA
www.opendoors.or.kr

Open Doors
PO Box 47
3850 AA Ermelo
THE NETHERLANDS
www.opendoors.nl

Open Doors
PO Box 27-630
Mt Roskill
Auckland 1030
NEW ZEALAND
www.opendoors.org.nz

Åpne Dører
Barstolveien 50 F
4636 Kristiansand
NORWAY
www.opendoors.no

Open Doors
PO Box 1573-1155
QCCPO Main
1100 Quezon City
PHILIPPINES

Open Doors
Raffles City Post Office
PO Box 150
Singapore 911705
REPUBLIC OF SINGAPORE
www.opendoors.org/ODS/index.
htm

Open Doors
Box 990099
Kibler Park 2053
Johannesburg
SOUTH AFRICA
www.opendoors.org.za

Puertas Abiertas
Apartado 578
28850 Torrejon de Ardoz
Madrid, SPAIN
www.puertasabiertas.org

Portcs Ouvertes
Case Postale 267
CH-1008 Prilly
Lausanne
SWITZERLAND
www.portesouvertes.ch/en

Open Doors
PO Box 6
Witney
Oxon 0X29 6WG
UNITED KINGDOM
www.opendoorsuk.org

Open Doors
PO Box 27001
Santa Ana, CA 92799
USA
www.opendoorsusa.org

STANDING STRONG THROUGH THE STORM

Paul Estabrooks and Jim Cunningham

We in the West are in a spiritual battle and we are losing it.
- Satan is the enemy of the Body of Christ. His aim is to destroy the Church and every Christian within it!
- The means (weapons) our adversary uses vary according to the situation each Christian faces.
- In different regions of the world there are Christians who are conquering Satan's attacks and living as victorious overcomers. They have learned how to "stand strong through the storm".

Learn the lessons from the Persecuted Church so we too can stand strong in the face of all that Satan is now throwing against us in the western world.

This material will increase your commitment and discipleship to Jesus Christ—and to the growth of His Church—as well as provide biblical preparation for the coming storms.

Available from Open Doors offices listed at the back of this book.

STANDING STRONG THROUGH THE STORM

More and more Christians around the world are becoming aware it is an illusion to believe biblical Christian living guarantees a trouble-free life. Jesus Himself said otherwise.

Overcoming victory is not the removal of suffering and persecution but standing strong in the midst of it.

Standing Strong Through the Storm guides you through the process and discovery of vital, biblical keys to becoming a Christian who can stand strong – and be victorious – no matter what the storm.

This is an excellent work. It is thorough, practical, well-supported biblically but also effectively illustrated from the experiences of the suffering people of God.

> — Terrance L. Tiessen, PhD, Professor of Systematic Theology,
> Providence College & Seminary, Otterburne, MB, Canada

Standing Strong Through the Storm *(SSTS) provides training for leadership in the Persecuted Church offering them instruction and counsel to face current and pending crises. I have shared in teaching the SSTS seminar and found it provides an excellent forum to share blessings and insights with one another in the service of Christ. This mutuality motivates the Body of Christ to press on in its evangelism and discipleship efforts. This book is recommended for believers in any country.*

> — Carlin Weinhauer, Pastor Emeritus,
> Willingdon Church, Burnaby, BC, Canada

Standing Strong Through the Storm *is very good material. It prepares us theoretically and practically for pressures and persecution that can come to any of us at any time. I wish this had been available in the 1960s when the Baptist Church in Russia experienced much conflict and suffering.*

> — Nikolai Popov, retired Russian pastor of the
> Unregistered Baptist Church who spent ten years in the Gulag

In my 35 years serving the Persecuted Church and travelling with Brother Andrew all over the world, I have had one great desire: "How can we effectively communicate the lessons we have learned from our persecuted brethren?" Well here you have it...an historic book! It will revolutionize your walk with the Lord.

> — Johan Companjen, President, Open Doors International

ABOUT THE AUTHOR

Paul Estabrooks is a veteran foreign missionary with a deep concern for Christians in restricted countries. He is the author of *SECRETS TO SPIRITUAL SUCCESS*, a volume documenting life lessons we can learn from those who have experienced "the lion's den." As well he has written a series of booklets and compiled a major training manual used around the world entitled *STANDING STRONG THROUGH THE STORM (SSTS)* for Christians experiencing or preparing for pressure and persecution. His latest booklet which introduces *SSTS* to the western world is titled, *RED SKIES @ DAWN.*

Estabrooks joined **Open Doors** in 1979 as Research Manager for the Asia region. **Open Doors** is a non-profit non-denominational organization founded by Brother Andrew. It distributes Bibles, brings encouragement, training and other assistance to Christians living in areas where they are persecuted or are restricted in living out or sharing their faith... encouraging them to reach out to others around them.

Prior to joining **Open Doors**, Estabrooks—whose roots are in Maritime Eastern Canada—served eight years with the **Far East Broadcasting Company** in Manila, Philippines as head of the Overseas Program Department. It was during these years of considerable travel throughout Asia that he developed an awareness and concern for Christians in spiritual need in countries like North Korea, China, Russia, Vietnam, Cambodia, India and Burma.

He was the project coordinator for Open Doors' **Project Pearl**—the delivery of one million Chinese Bibles (232 tons) on one night—June 18, 1981. Following the project, he served **Open Doors** for three years as Southeast Asia Coordinator—based in Singapore—as well as Director for Canada for five years.

As a representative of **Open Doors**, he has visited Christians in restricted countries as diverse as Cuba, Tibet, Iraq, China, Bhutan, Mongolia, Iran, India, the former Soviet Union and the Middle East. He has shared his experiences of meeting Persecuted Christians with numerous audiences in Europe, Australia, the Middle East, Asia, Africa, and South and North America.

Estabrooks graduated from **Tyndale University College** (LCBM - London, Ontario) in 1966 with a Bachelor of Theology degree. He later received a Bachelor and Master of Arts (with distinction) from **Wayne State University** in Detroit, Michigan majoring in Mass Communications.

He and his wife, Dianne, have been married for forty-one years. They have three grown children, seven grandchildren, and make their home in London, Ontario, Canada.

Contact by e-mail: paule@rogers.com

2014 POSTSCRIPT ADDENDUM

Since this book was written, there have been changes in the leadership of North Korea. None has made it any easier for our Christian brothers and sisters there. They continue to need our prayers.

North Korea was again Number One on the Open Door's World Watch List this past year for the twelfth year running. Kim Jong-Il died in the autumn of 2011 and was succeeded by his third son, Kim Jong-Un who at 31 years of age is the world's youngest head of state. His policies have made it even more difficult for Christians in the land.

The rule of Kim Jong-Un and his Workers' Party is absolute and strict. No one is allowed or able to challenge this rule. The ideology is based on Communist ideas, therefore, it is justified to name this as the main persecution engine. It is tied with an unimaginable personality cult. The country "exists" to serve the leaders. The God-like worship of the rulers leaves no room for any religion. Every reverence not concentrated on the Kim dynasty is seen as dangerous and state-threatening. Christians face the highest imaginable pressure.

They are pushed deeply underground, and in most cases, often do not dare show their Christian faith even in their own families out of fear that they will be revealed as Christians. Every entity the government is not able to control is removed, and therefore the underground churches remain as secret as possible. In each and every sphere of life, the pressure is of the highest level. All dissenters consistently testify that one would certainly be persecuted for practicing religion on a personal level. Christians are sent to political labor camps from which there is no release possible.

There are still an estimated 70,000 Christians in prison camps. North Korean police officials hunt down and vigorously prosecute North Koreans who convert to Protestant Christianity while in China or those who attempt to bring Christian literature, primarily Bibles or Scripture portions, back with them to North Korea.

Open Doors continues to minister to the more than 200,000 Christians in North Korea with Bibles, spiritual books, training and food and medical aid where needed. To find out how you can help, contact Open Doors at one of the addresses in your country noted in the back pages of this volume. Your prayers and support are vital.

Paul Estabrooks
February, 2014